FACING

YOUR FEARS

FACING YOUR FEARS

BIBLICAL INSIGHTS
FOR HOPE AND HEALING

THERESA ROTH

DEDICATION

To my mom, Lucile, who stood by my side when my
world came crashing down, and to my husband, David,
who unconditionally loved me through my healing
journey and then cheered me on to write my story.

CONTENTS

Prologue

SICK OF BEING SICK

In 1983, my husband, John, was killed in a terrorist attack while serving as a Marine officer in Beirut, Lebanon. I was 23 years old. This tragedy altered the trajectory of my life. For decades I ran from this experience and the pain that came with it.

That's when I began a practice I call "stuffing." Rather than face difficult emotions, I stuffed them inside. I pushed them down and packed them tight. I chose to ignore all the pain that came with losing John. Instead of dealing with it, I hoped it would just go away.

As a result, I was paralyzed with fear—fear of facing the hurt, fear of feeling the pain all over again, fear of conflict, fear of the unknown. I shut out friends and family, turned my back on religious teachings, and compartmentalized every emotion and interaction. As the years rolled by, I made new friends, reestablished some family ties, and strengthened my faith and relationship with God, but I continued to ignore the hurt (and collected more along the way), and my pain grew deeper. Eventually that unresolved pain affected my entire being—physically, emotionally, and even spiritually.

It wasn't until 2016, when extended bouts of sickness plagued me with little or no medical explanation, that I began to really look within myself and heavily lean on God. I was desperate for answers and began aggressively exploring ways to improve my physical health along with my emotional and spiritual well-being. My faith was growing into a much deeper dependence on God. Sickness had a way of focusing my attention on the fundamental aspects of life—when you're nauseated 24/7, regardless of whether you eat or not, it doesn't leave time to think about much else. I began fervently praying for God's wisdom and perspective on my situation. I didn't know what was causing my sickness or pain or how to get better, but I knew God did.

I spent countless hours crying out to the Lord through prayer, reading my Bible and many devotionals, journaling, and seeking wise counsel from spiritual teachers, therapists, and other professionals. I yearned for encouragement, strength, understanding, and direction. Through that process, I began to realize that stuffing my pain wasn't a way of processing, it was harming me. Ignoring my hurts and being afraid to address them was making matters worse—my physical, emotional, and spiritual health were all suffering.

After decades of stuffing, I decided to face my emotions and address the pain. I was no longer going to stuff. I was no longer going to be afraid. It was time to move forward.

Then a miraculous thing happened.

As I overcame my fears and faced my unresolved emotions, the pain that I so skillfully stuffed began to resolve. Recovery entered all aspects of my life, and the healing continues even to this day.

During that spiritual and emotional deep dive, I journaled extensively. I wrote down many biblical insights that helped and encouraged me—that gave me the courage to face all I'd stuffed, showed me God's faithfulness even in the difficulties, and provided evidence of his goodness and mercy and redemptive hand through it all.

I'm grateful that God led me to those insights. I held onto them throughout this process. God's strength carried me through, and he has shown me great comfort through the process. As a result, I have such empathy for others going through their own challenges of unresolved pain. I want to extend to you the same comfort God gave me.

It took me so long to start the journey—more than three decades. It didn't have to be that way. I believe that God's timing is perfect, and it is in his timing now that God has put on my heart to share these insights with you. If you're dealing with unresolved pain and fear, your path to healing can begin a lot sooner than mine. And, if you've already been avoiding processing your pain for years—or even decades—I want to help you move toward healing now.

There is Scripture that captures this beautifully, "Praise be to the God and Father of our Lord Jesus Christ, the Father of compassion and the God of all comfort, who comforts us in all our troubles, so that we can comfort those in any trouble with the comfort we ourselves receive from God" (2 Corinthians 1:3-4).

The pages that follow are my story and the biblical insights that inspired me to walk the path from fear to resilience, from suffering to health, from defeat to victory.

These are my memories, and mine alone. I share actions, conversations, and events as I remember them. Memory is imperfect, just as humans are imperfect, and—as I mentioned earlier—some of these memories are decades old. I've changed some of the names— sometimes to protect people's privacy, other times because we've lost touch and I don't know how they'd feel about being included. When you see dialogue, this is my recollection of the conversation. There are no transcripts to reference, and the words are not verbatim, but it's how they live in my memory and therefore how they influenced my journey and the insights I feel called to share.

My personal experiences and the spiritual insights I've gained are uniquely mine. I humbly acknowledge that I lack the formal education of a theologian, but I am a devoted follower of Jesus Christ.

While my perspectives are heartfelt, they may not resonate with every reader, and I respect that diversity. Through this book, I hope to extend a helping hand to others going through difficult challenges and offer them the guidance I found in my own journey of healing.

Although your story is different from mine, I pray these insights will inspire you to start your journey toward hope and healing.

Part I

THE STORY OF MY PAIN

Chapter 1

THE ATTACK

I was a typical kid—the youngest of five—living in a small town in south Georgia. My dad was a sales executive, and my mom was the secretary at our local Catholic school, where I also attended. For much of my childhood, I took dance and competed in gymnastics. As a teenager, I taught at the same dance studio where I spent many of my after-school hours.

It was there, in the summer after my sophomore year, where I met John. He was a couple of years older than me and had just graduated from my high school. His aunt, the studio's owner and lead dance instructor, recruited John and a couple of other guys to help with dance lifts for a routine that a few girls and I would perform later that summer. None of the guys were experienced dancers, but they were all athletic and his aunt's choreography took their inexperience into consideration. We all had a blast at the rehearsals, and the performance was a hit.

John and I hit it off, too.

We dated over the summer, but when school resumed the freshman-in-college and junior-in-high-school thing wasn't working, so we broke it off. However, after he returned home from college the next summer, we realized we didn't want to date anyone else. We were crazy about each other, and he became my high school sweetheart.

It was hard being apart when he went back to college. John attended South Dakota State University in Brookings, where he played football. We didn't see each other much, but we talked often, and we were inseparable whenever he was home. We made long-distance dating work for us.

When it was time to look ahead to college, I knew in my heart I wanted to be with John. I had considered attending other universities, but those thoughts were a thing of the past. I began to consider SDSU. When it was time to make a decision, somehow I convinced my parents that this Georgia girl would be fine in a whole different part of the country.

In August of 1978, John and I drove 1,400 miles to start this next chapter of our lives. For the next couple of years, we were busy doing the college thing. John was playing football, and I was a walk-on with the women's gymnastics team. Between our athletic commitments, classes, and fraternity and sorority activities, we were living full and active college lives as a couple—and we were having the time of our lives—and he proposed in December of 1979, when I was a sophomore and he was a senior.

In August 1980, we were married in our hometown at my Catholic church. It was a beautiful wedding, and many of our family members, local friends, and even friends from South Dakota were there to support us. We were John and Theresa Boyett, ready to take on the world.

John graduated that December, and we moved to Quantico, Virginia, in February 1981. Since he was a member of the Reserve Officers' Training Corps in college, John was commissioned as a second lieutenant in the Marine Corps and attended The Basic

School—known as TBS—for officer and leadership training.

I knew we would be moving around quite a bit as a military couple, so I decided to take a break from college. Getting a college education was still a goal for me even if it was delayed. It was important to me that at some point in the future I'd go back and finish my degree, but I wanted to be a supportive wife during this transition, so I felt good about the decision.

Life as an officer's wife was much like what I'd seen in the movies—that was the only exposure that I had to military life beyond knowing that my dad served in the Navy in World War II. While John trained at Quantico, I worked in a local military uniform retail store, met other wives, and attended officers' wives club functions. I even went to Washington, DC, and attended a gathering with several other wives at the Marine Corps commandant's home. I was having fun, and I liked this new lifestyle.

After John finished TBS, he received orders to report to Camp Lejeune Marine Base in Jacksonville, North Carolina, where we would be stationed for the next three years. Once there, he attended Ground Supply School and later was promoted to first lieutenant and assigned to the First Battalion, Eighth Marines (1/8) as their ground supply officer.

While we waited for officers housing to become available on base, we lived on Topsail Island for a few months. It was about a forty-five-minute drive from base, and we only owned one car. In the summer, I was in heaven since I loved the beach, but once the weather changed and the tourists left, I was really lonely. John left for work early each morning and arrived home in the evening, which meant I found myself alone for ten to twelve hours most days.

I was lonely and bored. I was an unhappy young wife, and I thought it was my husband's job to fix it—to make me happy. That's when I got some profound advice from my mom that I go back to often, even today.

"Theresa, no one can make you happy," she said. "*You* have to make yourself happy."

In April of 1982, a house became available on base. We moved and bought a second car, and I got a job at a store in the local mall. After that, we settled into a routine, and life was good again—two young people doing the adult married thing and adjusting to life on base as a military couple.

Just after we moved, I learned that the University of North Carolina at Wilmington was an hour away. My mom's advice was still ringing in my ears, and getting my college education was still important to me.

While I was kicking around the idea of returning to school, a friend told me her sister was getting a degree in computer science. I studied apparel design at SDSU, but when my friend shared that information technology was the latest thing in careers and in high demand, I realized how much easier it would be to find a job in that field, no matter where we lived. So I switched majors and determined that if I attended three semesters along with summer school, I could complete my degree and graduate in December 1983. That was the plan.

John worked, and I commuted to UNCW. I started classes in summer 1982, while still working at the store in the mall. I was back to my busy, non-stop, happy self once again. Mom's advice was spot on.

In May 1983, John's battalion was deployed to Beirut, Lebanon, on a multinational peacekeeping mission. He was part of the 24th Marine Amphibious Unit and the 1/8 Battalion Landing Team— known as the 24th MAU and the 1/8 BLT. Their mission was to be a presence of peace in the war-torn country.

I was concerned about his safety. When I shared this with my boss, he said that John had a greater chance of getting hurt or killed in a car accident than he did in Beirut. I felt no empathy from his weak attempt to reassure me, but I supposed there was some truth to his point and tried to use his observation to calm myself whenever I let worry set in.

The US multinational peacekeeping operation would reside on

the Beirut International Airport grounds. I was relieved to learn that John would be working and living in a four-story building on the property, which became the Marine Corps BLT Headquarters and barracks for the mission.

I was thankful that he wouldn't be with the troops who were working and living in tents and temporary buildings scattered around the grounds. They seemed the most vulnerable to sniper attacks, while I reassured myself that John would be protected by steel reinforcements, brick, and mortar.

As time went on, the peacekeeping mission didn't feel so peaceful. There were no cell phones or video calls to keep me informed in 1983, so I depended on the news and letters from John, which often took two to three weeks to reach me—the epitome of "snail mail." While the letters I received in the summer and fall talked about random sniper attacks and mortar attacks, I continued to remind myself that John was safe inside a steel-reinforced building.

I kept going to class, working at the mall, and living my life. Before John was deployed we had gotten a dog, Winston, who also kept me occupied. There were other wives I'd gotten to know whose husbands were also deployed. Some of the wives were still on base, and we spent time just hanging out together. Others went home to be with family, and I talked to them regularly on the phone. Just as I learned the role of being an officer's wife, I was adapting to a new normal of having a husband deployed overseas.

On the morning of October 23, 1983, I awoke to a frantic phone call from the wife of another Marine officer who was on the mission with John.

"Theresa, turn on your TV," she said. "There has been a bombing."

I stood in front of my TV and stared at what used to be a four-story building—the building that I knew John worked and lived in. On the screen was a pile of rubble made of the steel, brick, and mortar that I thought would protect my husband. The floor and room that I knew he would've been sleeping in were destroyed. I screamed. I fell to my knees, and the reality of the situation came crashing down on me.

John was gone.

I later learned that a civilian truck loaded with 12,000 pounds of explosives had circled the airport grounds several times without causing suspicion. The airport was still operational, so no one questioned a civilian truck driving around the property. After a few laps, it turned toward the Marine Corps BLT barracks, sped up, ran through several barricades, and crashed into the building, detonating the explosives on board. The force of the explosion lifted the building from its foundation and caused it to implode.

It was reported to be the largest non-nuclear explosion the world had seen before 9/11, and it began the war on terrorism that we're still fighting today.

Frantically, I tried to call my parents, but I learned that they were on separate trips. Dad was at a family reunion in Florida, and Mom was attending a National Council of Catholic Women Convention in Denver.

I was alone with the shock and terror of this horrendous act. Many of the details of the days following the attack are fuzzy, at best, while others I've never been able to recall.

I remember that my mom arrived at some point in the first 24-48 hours. When she returned from her Denver trip, she was met at the airport gate in Atlanta and told the news. She jumped on the next available flight to be with me. I had never needed my mom more.

I felt numb. I couldn't get enough sleep. I know now that sleep was my way of coping, but at the time all I knew was that even after ten or twelve hours of sleep I still wanted—I still needed—more.

A few days after my mom arrived, the doorbell rang in the middle of the night. I immediately knew what that meant, so I grabbed a robe and walked to the front door with my mom. Just like I'd seen in the movies, a Casualty Assistance Officer—known as CAO—stood in his dress uniform with a solemn look on his face. I happened to know the Marine standing in front of me. 1st Lt. Paul Bennett was a peer of John's. He and his wife were our friends.

Somehow we got from the doorway into the living room. "Have a seat," he said.

As a CAO, Lt. Bennett had a job to do, and he needed to do it without emotion. But as a friend, I can't imagine the dread and sorrow Paul felt. To deliver such heartbreaking news must have taken immense strength.

My mom held my hand and tried to prepare me to hear the news. My heart was pounding, my stomach was in my throat, and I had an overwhelming feeling of doom. But what came next was unexpected.

"John is missing," Paul said.

Paul explained that John had not been identified, and all the Marine Corps could tell me at that point was that he was unaccounted for. He was missing in action—MIA.

What in the world? So where was John?

Over the next few days, news reports said that some servicemen had been rescued from the rubble and rushed to hospitals in surrounding countries. I wondered if John had survived the bombing, and I became hopeful, despite the reality of the situation, that maybe, just maybe, he was still alive.

The Marine Corps family was very supportive. People brought food and came by to check on me. Military personnel stopped in to assist me with financial accounts, legal documents, and all the paperwork that comes with having a missing spouse. It was clear that the Marines took care of their own in trying times.

I have vague memories of attending a ceremony on base for families, spouses, and survivors of the attack. I recall standing in an airport hangar and being personally greeted by President Reagan and his wife, Nancy, who were there to offer their support and concern. It was cold, raining, and dreary—like the emotions I felt.

For decades, I wasn't sure if that actually had happened or if I dreamed it. When I began to write this book, I finally had the courage to find out, and I confirmed that, in fact, it did take place. On November 4, 1983, President and Mrs. Reagan were in attendance—and so was I.

Even after that memorial service, I continued to hang on to hope. John remained classified as MIA, and I prayed that he was still alive somewhere and they couldn't identify who he was for some reason. My imagination went crazy.

Maybe his dog tags blew off in the explosion. Maybe he had amnesia. Perhaps he couldn't talk. Perhaps he was in a coma.

For a while I remained hopeful, but as the days stretched on, my hope began to dwindle.

One evening, while I was taking a bath and lying in the tub for a long while, I had a strong sense that John was truly gone. I felt it in my soul. I even prayed to God—really, it was more like a threat than a prayer—that he'd better put John in someone else's body because I couldn't be on this Earth by myself. I was 23 years old—much too young to be a widow.

A few hours later, in the middle of the night, the doorbell rang—and I knew.

Once again, our friend Paul appeared in his dress uniform. Again, he told me to have a seat. Then he told me what no wife ever wants to hear.

"Theresa, I'm sorry, but John's body was found and identified, and he was in fact killed in the terrorist attack."

I was numb.

My mom and I flew back to my hometown of Albany, Georgia, to begin funeral preparations and be with John's and my family. My first task was to go to the funeral home. I was asked to pick out a casket, tombstone, and burial plot. I just sat there, speechless. I was trying to respond like a grown-up.

What 23-year-old goes through this?

I was still a kid who wanted somebody to help me. I wanted to scream, "Please don't make me make these decisions!"

Paul also traveled to Albany, and he was by my side, once again, and thank God I had somebody who was thinking clearly to help guide me through these decisions.

Two memories have stuck with me from those days, and both involve the arrival and identification of John's body.

John's remains had been transported across the ocean, and I wanted to be at the airport when the plane arrived. As I stood at the gate, I saw a flag-draped casket coming out of the plane and several uniformed servicemen on the runway.

This wasn't the way I pictured my husband's return. Instead of the homecoming of hugs and kisses that kept me going all those months while he was deployed, there he was—in a box. There are no words.

My second memory is after John's body arrived at the funeral home. I was asked, "Theresa, would you like to see the body?"

There was a long pause after the question as I fought an un-winnable internal battle.

Do I see him in whatever condition he was in to see for myself that it was, in fact, John? Do I decline because I don't want that to be my last memory?

Before I was able to process my response, Paul jumped in.

"Let me, Theresa," he said. "Don't let that be your last memory of John. Let me do that for you."

What an incredible act of selflessness. Mental images can last forever. We can never *unsee* something. This man, John's friend, and my friend, carries that image *for me* to this day.

Because I didn't have that closure myself, for years I had random dreams of John showing up on my doorstep saying that he'd lost his memory and was just returning home. As time went by, those dreams changed to him saying, "Why didn't you wait for me?"

I've been told that this is a normal response when not seeing a loved one's body. Even though his identity had been confirmed through blood tests, dental records, and a visual confirmation, my subconscious mind didn't want to believe it. Thankfully, it's been a long time since I've had those dreams. I suppose my subconscious finally caught up with my reality.

The funeral took place on November 11, 1983, and the church was packed. I've been told that hundreds of people were in attendance, but I have no recollection of the service itself. For years, I thought about how strange the mind is in how it works to protect itself from traumatic experiences. Now, I see it as more evidence of our divine design.

After the funeral, our out-of-town family and friends traveled back to their homes. Everyone else went back to work and to their lives, and reality set in.

Where did that leave me? Alone.

Now what?

Oh, yeah, I was in the last semester of my senior year at UNCW. And I was taking a 21-hour course load. That's seven classes. I'd already missed several weeks, and I had no idea how I would pick up the pieces.

How could I possibly graduate on time?

Although I was emotionally drained, somehow I found the will to finish. That comment my mom made to me many months before kept coming to mind. I had to make myself happy, and I realized I needed that college education now more than ever.

I took on a philosophy that had been shared with me by so many during that time, "Pull yourself up by those bootstraps." I translated that into "Be a good soldier, Theresa. No time to deal with what just happened. Stuff your emotions and move on."

I had work to do.

So I returned to my home on Camp Lejeune and to Winston, who'd been cared for while I was gone. I talked to my professors to tell them what had happened. Of course, they already knew. This was a major international event, and they were told that John had been killed. Their kindness and understanding didn't change the fact that finals were approaching and final projects were due. I'd missed nearly a month of class. I had so much to make up and no clue how I was going to get to the finish line. My tank was empty.

Much to my relief and surprise, my professors and classmates pulled me through. Most professors excused my missed tests. Some told me they'd use my grade before the bombing occurred as my final grade. Others helped me through the final exam by sitting with me as I took it. They answered my questions, and we talked through anything I found confusing. One of the students in my most challenging class showed up one day and said he'd done all the research for my final project. All I had to do was write the paper.

Like much of late 1983, these last weeks of class are a bit foggy, but with help from many, along with my own hard work, I finished all my exams, projects, and essays.

In December 1983, I graduated with a double major in business management and computer science. I completed two years of college—with a new major—in eighteen months.

I chose not to attend my graduation. I was drained and didn't know if I had it in me. Looking back, I wish I'd gone. It was a significant milestone in my life, but it didn't feel the same without John. I ran from the experience and all the emotions that came with it— just like I would begin to run from everything in my life.

There I was, a college graduate, a widow, and—for all intents and purposes—homeless. I had to figure out my life.

So many questions ran through my mind. Who was I now that I was no longer married? Where would I live since I could no longer live on base? And what does a young widow do?

I had a big fat hole in my life. I was heartbroken and devastated. Everything about me was off kilter. I just wanted to be Theresa—to be treated like I was before this all happened.

In the midst of my sorrow I thought, *Thank God, I finished school.*

Thank God, I was led to return to college even before any of this happened. Thank God, I can support myself. But, even with all the things I was grateful for, there was one painful, blinding fact—John was gone. I was all alone.

Many people supported me in the days and weeks following the bombing, but the next phase of the journey was much more lonely. I began to sense that people were uncomfortable with me and my situation. It felt like they didn't know what to say, so they just avoided me.

Whenever I talked about John's death, people were so uneasy that I could see it on their faces and in their body language. It also came through in the platitudes they used to attempt to comfort me. Many of them said things that not only weren't empathetic, but some crossed a line into harmful.

They said things like, "It was just his time," "I know how you feel," "These things happen for a reason," "He's in a better place," and on, and on.

A word of advice: Don't ever say these things to someone in pain. It isn't helpful. It may make you feel better, but these statements often minimize the person's grief and they aren't a comfort to those who have recently lost someone they love.

The truth is, there really isn't anything you can say to make someone feel better. Just let your presence, concern, and care speak for itself.

This tragic experience showed me that few people know how to deal with death or how to comfort those left behind. I know I'm guilty of saying something well-meaning but ill-timed.

What I yearned to hear was simply "I'm sorry," along with a hug. All I wanted was people to be present with me in my sorrow.

However, what was even worse than the insensitive remarks was when someone wouldn't acknowledge that anything had happened. Instead, they'd ignore me, or they'd see me and not say a word about what I was going through—like it never happened.

These ill-timed comments, actions, and avoidance all were like daggers to my broken heart and mind.

After I finished college, I returned to Albany. Christmas was approaching. Sometimes I felt similar reactions when people saw me while I was home. I wasn't mature enough to understand how uncomfortable death makes people—and how they might react to that discomfort. It was hard not to be hurt or offended. Plus, I honestly didn't know how to deal with my own emotions—grief, anger, bitterness, fear, shock, and hopelessness—or even what to do with them.

In my immature and grief-stricken state, I decided that everyone was a whole lot better off if I kept my sadness, confusion, horror, and anger to myself—to just remain silent, to stuff what happened, and run from my brutal reality.

I also couldn't handle being called a "widow" at such a young age. That term freaked me out. No one explicitly told me how I needed to live or how to grieve John, but the term "widow" brought up the vision of me as an old woman. I felt like I was expected to live an old person's life—like I was already in my eighties. The idea of facing the years ahead of me alone and heartbroken haunted me.

I wish someone would've taken me under their wing and told me that what I was experiencing was grief, trauma, and shock and those things take time to work through. I wasn't only suffering from the trauma that happened to me, but also the impact that it was having in me. My well-being—how I felt, how I thought, how I functioned—was impacted more than I even realized at the time. This was a seriously traumatic event that just happened. The entire world was changed, not to mention my life.

Looking back, I find it interesting that no one ever suggested counseling. It just wasn't something many people did in the early 1980s. People didn't voluntarily talk about their feelings, and no one encouraged me to talk about them either. So, I assumed, the quicker I recovered, the better—for my sake and for the sake of everyone around me. The best way forward was to never look back and to stuff all my complicated emotions, hoping they'd eventually go away on their own.

I had my plan and a degree; now I needed a job and a place to live. I wanted to be anonymous, to be around people who didn't know me, didn't know about John's death, and wouldn't remind me of who and what I'd lost. I wanted to ignore the big, fat hole in my heart. So I had to wrestle with a new question.

Where do I go now?

Chapter 2

STUFFING MY PAIN

Staying in North Carolina wasn't an option. John was gone. I couldn't remain on base as a civilian, but I didn't even want to stay in the state without him. There were so many reminders of him, our life together, and even his death. Moving back to Albany didn't make sense either, because it was our hometown. I couldn't bear that he was no longer alive, and that all the places we used to go and the people we used to hang out with were reminders that he was gone.

I decided it was best to move to a new city, but rather than seeing this decision as running *to* what was next, I was running *from* what would never be again. I decided to run away from my life, from my family, from John's family, and from any reminders of him—just run.

Fortunately, my dad's boss—the company owner—had connections to a bank headquartered in Atlanta. Dad asked if he'd find out if the bank had any job opportunities. Sure enough, they had an opening in the information technology department, and I got an interview for an entry-level job. I was grateful for that connection and a foot in the door. I didn't have the energy to beat the bushes and find a job on my own in my newfound career.

As I prepared my resume for the interview, I dreaded the questions I thought they might ask: Why did you attend a university in South Dakota so far away from home? What took you to North Carolina?

My resume was loaded with potential questions that would lead me to discussing John's death and the tragedy that I just experienced. I didn't want these new people to feel uncomfortable with me right off the bat, so I quickly became an expert in dancing around the truth—a skill I carried with me for decades, and frankly, an exhausting habit that's hard to break.

During the interview, I discovered they had a six-month training program in their technology department. I was relieved because even though my degree was in computer science and business management, I had no clue what I was supposed to do with that. A training program would be perfect. After the interview, they offered me a job, and I quickly accepted.

Moving away from almost everyone and everything that reminded me of life with John seemed like the best and easiest thing to do. I didn't know anyone in Atlanta except my sister, Margaret, who lived there with her family. I didn't have to worry about her reaction to me. She was safe and always supportive—a great big sister. I realized I could be anonymous to everyone else and start over. I could leave my broken heart behind.

I packed up Winston, our home at Camp Lejeune, and life as I knew it. John and I were married for only three years, so we hadn't accumulated much. As I went through his belongings, deciding what to keep and what to give away was challenging. Memories surrounded each of his things. Even though I gave away most of his clothing, I made sure to keep a box of his more personal items, including letters, medals, awards, and correspondence.

I put it all in a moving box, sealed it with packing tape, and marked it with his name. It wasn't big, about twelve-by-sixteen inches, and it wasn't heavy—at least not physically. That box moved with me for thirty-five years—unopened. As I think now about that box, I realize I also included a part of me—all the emotions and pain I experienced from his death. I stuffed that box with his things the same way I stuffed my emotions. As time passed, I was afraid to open it and face all the memories and the emotions that went with them.

In Atlanta, I threw myself into my new job and started a new life. I went through the training program and found out pretty quickly that the life of a programmer wasn't for me. I wanted to work more closely with people—to help them. So, after a business associate left the bank to go to a large software company, I found myself asking about a job there. I was looking for something more in alignment with my skills and personality.

As luck would have it, they had a job opening in their customer service department. I would work with clients who had questions about or issues with the software they purchased. Rather than writing the software, I would help people who were using the software, which was right up my alley.

My career took off, and a few years and several promotions later, I'd worked my way up the corporate ladder of this $84 million company. I was a division director surrounded by mostly male peers. I had a staff of six consultants and a travel schedule that often took me across the United States and Canada, and even to Australia and Europe. It felt like I had my professional life under control, but that was far from the truth for my personal life.

My faith was dormant. Aside from our Catholic wedding and attending mass when I visited home, I'd abandoned my religious upbringing after going to college. It's not that I didn't believe in God. I just wasn't actively practicing my faith. I couldn't see past the ritual and understand that there was also a rich relationship with God that I was missing. As a result, I assumed that anything negative in my life was because God was punishing me for some past sin that I must have committed, and who wants to hang out with a God who punishes them for every wrong move?

Doubt, fear, and unresolved emotions consumed me. I had no clue that I needed to seek guidance or where to find it. My moral compass was based on what seemed best in the moment rather than what was best for me long-term. I didn't want to manage drama or confrontation, so I did whatever was easy or fun or most agreeable to others. I was floating through life, determined to avoid decisions and negative emotions because I'd already had enough of both for a lifetime. As a result, I was riddled with wrong love interests and made many poor, misguided decisions.

Before I was thirty years old, I'd checked all the boxes when asked if I was single, married, widowed, or divorced.

Divorced, you ask? Yep. I remarried in 1986, three years after John was killed, but it didn't last. I guess you could call it a rebound marriage.

Remember the night I found out that John was dead and I prayed that God would bring him back to me in someone else? Well, when I met the man who later became my second husband, there were "signs" that I chose to believe. He shared the same birthday as John. He had one sibling, just like John. He was even born in the same town as John. I convinced myself that somehow he *was* John, but of course he wasn't, and that wasn't his fault. We parted ways a couple of years later.

I felt even more lost and broken after that experience. Since I saw myself as lost and broken, I assumed that was how everyone else saw me. I'd adopted it as part of my identity, and even if someone had tried to convince me otherwise, I would've brushed any comments aside.

Along with all the emotions I worked so hard to stuff, I could now add another to the mix—shame. I was already determined to not share my story since death made people uncomfortable. Now, I didn't want to share my latest story because of my failure. If people knew everything about me now—including that I was divorced—they would also view me as bad or flawed in addition to lost or broken.

My shame deepened my commitment to keep my past hidden. I wasn't proud of my divorce—and I'm still not proud of it today, but at least now I know it didn't make me a bad person.

Now I realize that I was young, vulnerable, and carrying around unresolved pain, but that's not how I saw it back then. So many people have gone through rebound marriages that have ended in divorce. I now understand God extended me grace and mercy for my failed marriage, but I certainly didn't grant it to myself, or see it coming from God, at the time.

Once I embraced stuffing my emotions, I began to hone and nurture that skill. Instead of facing my failed marriage—and another failed relationship after that—I continued to stuff it all and ignore the emotional toll it was taking.

By age thirty, I remember thinking, it was time to accept being alone and be okay with that. I distinctly recall being on a flight from Los Angeles after a business trip and feeling defeated, lost, and alone. I wanted to be loved, but judging by my past relationships, that wasn't meant to be.

It was on that flight when I surrendered to God and silently cried out, "God, I'm finally ready to just be alone. I'm tired of looking for love, and I'll be okay not having it."

That was my plan, but God had a different one.

Since I wanted to keep my private life and my secrets of sadness to myself, I purposefully didn't mix my personal and business worlds. Very few people at work knew my entire story. It was more manageable, less uncomfortable that way—for them and for me.

There was a man I occasionally worked with who was such a nice guy—handsome too. David and I were business associates, and nothing more. I made sure of that mostly because of my personal/business rule, but also because every young, single woman in our company swooned over him, and I was *not* going to get caught up in that drama. Swooning and rules aside, he was a wonderful, kind-hearted man. He was a business consultant in a different department, and over the past couple of years, we had become professional friends, and that was all I was interested in.

As God would have it, David and I were assigned to a project a couple months after that Los Angeles flight, and we began to work more closely. One day, I was walking down the hall to my office, and I had a vision that came out of nowhere. David and I were walking together, each holding a hand of a child between us. It stopped me in my tracks. I leaned against the wall to regain my composure. My mind was swirling.

What in the world? Where did that come from?

I brushed the vision aside, regained my composure, and went about my day.

A few weeks later, David called and asked if he could come to my office to talk with me. Since we were working on that project together, I didn't think twice about it.

When he showed up, he sat down and said, "Theresa, would you like to start seeing each other outside of the company?"

I was caught totally off guard. I had declared a few months earlier in prayer to God that it was time to be alone. Before I could think about my firm personal/business boundary, I said, "Yes!" and became downright giddy.

On February 10, 1991, we had our first date.

Since we already knew each other, we didn't have to go through the typical awkward conversations, and our first date was more like spending time with a good friend. It lasted twelve hours. We jogged along the river, attended a church service, walked around and threw a Frisbee at Piedmont Park, and watched a college basketball game—and we talked the entire time.

Of course, I didn't say a word about my past. No need. It was the best-kept secret, right?

A few dates later, while David and I were driving around, he said, "Theresa, I've heard that you've had a tragedy in your life. Is that true?"

I hesitantly said yes.

"Would you tell me about it?" he said.

"Do you *really* want to know?" I said. Others had asked me the same question, and when I answered, I could see the dust in their tracks when they ran the other way.

But not David.

"Yes," he said. "I want to know *everything*."

I knew then that David was someone special, and that maybe, just maybe, he'd accept my past, be okay with my secrets of sadness, and offer empathy and love regarding the horrors in my past.

And he did.

No matter what I told him, he just listened. No judgment. No abandonment. Total acceptance. And even tears. My naïve prayer when John died about God placing him in someone else's body? I didn't have those thoughts this time.

This was David, and we began to fall head over heels for each other.

Our romance was whirlwind. We were inseparable—we worked together, often traveled on business together, and spent our free time together. After our first date in February, we were engaged on July 4, and on October 5, 1991, I became Theresa Roth. David was thirty-four years old, and I was thirty-one.

I had found someone I could love and who loved me back— unconditionally. He knew all of my story and loved me not in spite of what I'd been through, but rather—at least in part—*because* of it. He never saw me as broken. He saw someone who'd survived a tragedy and come out the other side.

Since that incredible day in 1991 when David asked to know *everything*, we've built a life together. We've had two amazing boys, Dylan and Tyler, moved from Atlanta to Maryland and then to

Arkansas, and celebrated more than thirty years of marriage.

Looking back, I realize it wasn't until I surrendered my personal life to God—the part *I* labeled as broken—that he'd work *his* plan for my life. I got out of God's way, and *his* plan began to unfold, in *his* timing and in *his* ways. Yes, it was well with my soul. I could finally put my past behind me.

I wish I could say that those emotions I had so skillfully stuffed disappeared at this point, too, but unfortunately, they didn't. I hadn't surrendered those to God yet. I've learned you can't carry around unresolved grief without its taking a toll. Unresolved emotions don't just disappear on their own—even while you're building a beautiful life with a wonderful partner. The old saying "time heals all wounds" is inaccurate. Yes, time has some healing qualities, but if you don't work through unresolved issues, then the pain continues.

Oh, you wouldn't have known it if you looked at me or even talked to me. I did a decent job of hiding it—from others and even from myself. It's incredible what the mind will do to protect itself. Just like a mom forgets the pain of childbirth, I "forgot" the pain of a traumatic death and the pain of a failed marriage. I thought my life with David would just erase all that.

Somewhere deep inside was a mess waiting to come out. Ignoring your emotions doesn't work—no matter how badly you want it to. I chose to deal with challenging situations going forward just like I handled my painful circumstances in my past. No matter how big or small a problem, I dealt with it by stuffing, ignoring, and avoiding—hoping it would fix itself.

Marriage, raising children, work, and doing life with others will always have its share of ups and downs. Conflicts, everyday challenges, frustrations, whatever, I handled them all the same—just stuff it, and it'll go away on its own. It didn't matter if that issue was with my family, friends, or coworkers, rather than having the courage to discuss and work through a problem, I ignored it, stuffed any painful emotions, and hoped that time would heal it.

Oh, how I wish I would've done the work to figure out how to face these painful emotions and learn how to resolve conflict and address old wounds. I wish I'd learned to identify my feelings and been courageous enough to reveal them and committed to solving them.

Instead, I chose temporary comfort over dealing with any of it. Looking back, what frustrates me the most is that it's not like I knew what to do and just refused to address it. I honestly believed that time would eventually make all the old hurts go away. While I say that I wish I'd had the courage, I was operating out of ignorance more than cowardice.

Even the idea of getting counseling—which seems like an obvious choice today—didn't cross my mind until I was in my fifties. I didn't think of it, nor was it suggested. I didn't know I had a way out of this hole I was stuck in. To be fair, I didn't let on to anyone that I was even in a hole until I had no other option.

For decades, I wore a mask that everyone else saw. That was the Theresa everyone knew. Even with David's example of empathy and acceptance, I was still afraid that if anyone knew the things that I really felt or the painful and even traumatic situations I had experienced, they would run the other way. I believed they'd tell me that I was weak and broken, that I had no reason to feel the emotions I had buried. I'd convinced myself to hold it all in and not reveal anything, and the longer I stuffed, the harder it was to open up.

Chapter 3

UNPACKING MY PAIN

The hard part of my story was that the longer I stuffed my emotions and avoided addressing difficult experiences, the bigger the burdens became. They were a huge weight deep within my soul. Just like things in the dark are a lot scarier than in the light, the same is true for emotions and pain you choose to bury. They get bigger and seem more frightening when left unresolved.

This pain that I buried was like a time bomb. What would it take to finally be willing to dig up all this pain and resolve it? Sometimes it takes getting to a place of desperation.

David, the boys, and I moved to Arkansas in 1999. Shortly after we arrived, I started to have some crazy health problems. Even though they were difficult to endure in the moment, they were later comical to describe. They were so bizarre that people started saying things like, "Theresa, you are that one in a million who will have an adverse reaction to anything."

I had a recluse spider bite that went haywire, causing trips to my primary doctor, a surgeon, and a dermatologist. I had an extended battle with night-time hives covering my body due to an allergic reaction to an electric blanket. I had a weird, lingering flu-like episode after a reaction to snorkeling with microscopic thimble jellyfish during a trip to Mexico. I was even rushed by ambulance to the ER after an unexplained swollen tongue and difficulty breathing.

Episodes like these went on for a few years. I recovered from each health challenge, and they became part of my bizarre tales that entertained many.

In 2005, my health issues became more serious. I began having pain in my lower back. It was so intense that it reminded me of the back labor I experienced when I had my first son, Dylan. I went to my primary doctor, and he recommended a CT scan. The tests showed a tumor lodged between my pancreas, liver, and aorta. My doctor wasn't sure if it had anything to do with my back pain, but he felt strongly that we should at least do a biopsy to determine if the growth was cancerous.

The tumor's location made the biopsy difficult, and it was ultimately unsuccessful. I couldn't stand the idea of leaving it inside my body, especially without knowing if it was cancer. We met with several local surgeons, but they all said the surgery to remove it would be dangerous.

To our surprise, the original radiologist who read the CT called us. He suggested that we seek another medical opinion elsewhere and recommended that we set up a consultation with a doctor at Baylor Hospital in Dallas. After lots of prayers, we decided to take his advice. The doctor at Baylor agreed that the tumor needed to be removed and recommended a surgeon he knew to do the procedure. Although it was a bit tricky, the surgery went well. The tumor was non-cancerous, and my back pain disappeared.

I was grateful for another positive health outcome—and it became another crazy story to share—but more health challenges were in store.

In 2008, my lower back started to hurt again. This time, it hurt so much that I couldn't sit for more than 15-30 minutes—car rides, working at a desk, and watching Tyler's basketball games became impossible (I was the mom pacing rather than sitting in the bleachers, and not because I was anxious about the score). The pain was intense when I was lying down, too, so sleep was difficult. I went to a couple of neurosurgeons. I got a base MRI, which led to two completely different diagnoses.

One doctor said I needed immediate back surgery. The other said it wasn't my back but my hip, and all I needed was some physical therapy. I took the advice of the second neurosurgeon.

After nine months of therapy, the pain was still there. I could barely walk to the mailbox, and my sleep was practically non-existent. I was miserable.

A friend, whose son was on Tyler's basketball team, was an orthopedic surgeon. I told him about my situation, and he suggested I seek another opinion. I made an appointment to see a third neurosurgeon who'd been highly recommended. He ordered a second MRI and confirmed that there was, in fact, an issue with my lower back. It was a herniated disc.

On a side note, that same neurosurgeon asked me if I was having neck pain, shoulder pain, or tingling in my hands. I told him no.

"Oh, you will," he said. "Not sure when, but you will. Your neck is even worse than your lower back."

I ignored that comment since I was more concerned about my immediate pain than in any predicted future discomfort. I promptly began doing the right exercises and physical therapy for my herniated disc. Over several months, my pain subsided. I was able to sit and stand and, thank God, sleep. In the summer of 2009, I even walked a 5K with my family. What a victory that was. Again, I believed all my pain was behind me.

In 2012, the third neurosurgeon's prediction about experiencing pain from the mess in my neck came true. I was stretching my back, and I felt my shoulder pop. It immediately started to hurt. I thought I might have somehow injured my rotator cuff.

Goodness, is this what happens when you get older? I was just stretching, for God's sake.

It got worse over a few days, and I lost the ability to lift my arm. I made an appointment with my orthopedic surgeon friend. He ordered an MRI, which revealed that my shoulder wasn't the problem. Guess what the issue was. Yep, my neck. Back to my neurosurgeon I went.

Ugh.

He wasn't surprised to see me since he'd seen trouble brewing years before. He ordered a cervical MRI, and after reading it, he told me I had three severely compressed cervical discs. The signals to the nerve in my shoulder were impinged, causing my inability to lift my arm. I was on the road to emergency three-level fusion surgery unless the neurosurgeon could see some rapid improvement in my arm movement.

He recommended that I begin doing some traction treatment and gave me a home cervical traction machine. In a matter of days, my arm showed slight improvement, which allowed me to postpone the surgery. It took nine months of physical therapy before I could lift my arm over my head again, but I managed to stay away from major surgery.

Sweet victory!

As if the neck and back issues weren't enough to deal with, in between all of that, I started having severe stomach issues. I began to feel like I had a knife just below my sternum, and there was a burning sensation that felt like an internal volcano.

All the traditional medical tests didn't reveal any issues, so I started seeing a naturopathic doctor who ordered lots of food sensitivity tests and determined that I was sensitive to gluten. I curbed my gluten intake and gradually got better.

Case solved.

In 2014, my stomach symptoms resurfaced. Rather than going to my regular doctor, I went straight to my naturopathic doc. This time the culprit was rice. Did you know that rice has trace amounts of arsenic? Ever so slight. She suggested that since I was eating gluten-free products that were rice-based, I may have inadvertently exposed myself to too much arsenic.

I immediately stopped eating anything that had rice as an ingredient, and in two weeks I was good as new. Go figure. Yet another weird Theresa health situation.

I found myself in a healthy season starting in 2015. I was experiencing a much-needed reprieve. Life was finally back to normal. But, even though I was physically well, I was afraid a new illness would show its face, and that concern was always lurking in the back of my mind. It wasn't so much *if* I'd be sick again but *when.*

David had been regularly meeting with a spiritual mentor, Tim, for the past few years. As they talked about their personal lives, David often updated Tim about me, our kids, and even my health issues. At some point in their conversations, David confidentially shared with Tim my personal story concerning John's death in the terrorist attack and how I stuffed the pain and emotions caused from that event.

In one of their meetings in early 2016, as David updated Tim about my recurrent health struggles, Tim made a comment that David later shared with me. Tim suggested that the pain I chose to stuff could potentially be unhealthy to me emotionally *and* physically.

Initially, I was offended. I felt he was implying that I was responsible for my health challenges—that these physical issues were my fault.

Even though I was put off by what he said, I began to ask myself if all these years of physical challenges might be related to ignoring the difficult things that had happened to me and stuffing my emotions. I remembered reading a devotional about stepping out of a boat. It didn't mean much to me when I first read it, but in the light of Tim's comment, it resonated with me in a new way.

I was starting to sense that I needed to dig through all the pain I'd stuffed for so many years. I had to open up and start unpacking all the emotions if I wanted to heal my old wounds. It was a process of self-awareness that I'd never even considered.

My quiet time of Bible reading and prayer increased exponentially when—since I had no idea what to do—I started praying and asking God to reveal his desires for me. Through deep time with the Lord, all the hurts that I'd buried over all the years started to resurface.

Oh, the pain!

I felt like the scales were falling from my eyes, and I began to really feel my feelings. I was experiencing so many emotions—fear, anger, grief, sorrow, shame, regret, bitterness, and resentment.

For someone like me who'd expertly stuffed everything that caused any difficult emotions, I didn't know how to resolve them once they returned to the surface. So I just let them sit there and simmer. They were in my full view, but I had no idea what to do with them or how to deal with them.

In the summer of 2016, before Tyler's high school senior year, my health took another turn for the worse. Those dang stomach issues reappeared. This time, it dragged on for months, and it was more severe. I was so incredibly nauseated. All. The. Time. Yuck.

I dropped thirty pounds in three months. I weighed less than I did when I was in eighth grade. So I did what I'd done in the past. I went to both traditional and alternative health experts. I searched for the reason for and solution to my illness. I was so miserable that I eliminated gluten, dairy, coffee, alcohol, and anything else I thought might be causing me to feel sick. But it didn't matter what I ate or if I ate, I just felt horrible.

No one had any answers. No one and nothing was healing me. I'd run out of options, and I was desperate—desperate enough to start unpacking.

I began searching beyond the physical and started looking into emotional issues. For the first time in my life, I was willing to get out of my comfort zone and find another solution. I was that sick. I was ready to become vulnerable and let others into my struggles, to learn from their experiences and seek their insight and expertise.

David and I were launching into uncharted territory, having never considered anything beyond the physical issues and seeking medical expertise. I realize now that we had no idea what we were taking on, but it became clear that I needed to deal with all the emotions I'd collected and stuffed down for so many years.

Could it be that all that unresolved pain was eating me up from the inside out?

That's when my spiritual journey got a lot more intense. Even though years earlier, I'd renewed my faith in God and developed a deep, personal relationship with Jesus, my unresolved illness and desperation took me to my knees. I was at a level of dependence on God that I hadn't experienced before.

So I went to the Great Physician, the Great Healer. Jesus and I became tight, and I prayed for God's wisdom and discernment, to get *his* perspective on my situation and to surround myself with his Word.

No one had an answer, but God did. No one could heal me, but God could. If I felt hopeless, God's Word and his promises would provide me hope. Even when I felt alone, I knew I wasn't because God was with me—and had always been.

Slowly, on my path toward healing through hours of prayer, reading my Bible and devotionals, and seeking spiritual counsel, I began to see things more from God's perspective. I began to understand that he cared more about my character than my comfort.

I also learned from hours of counseling that to clean out those wounds, as painful as it was, I had to unpack all my unresolved emotions that I'd stuffed so many years ago, starting with John's tragic death. It was crucial to open up and look inside every corner—any place I might have skillfully hidden or tucked away an unruly feeling.

I had to deal with those emotions that were simmering just under the surface and the events that led to them and let them heal. It was time to name the feelings I felt and process through each of them, and as I did, my emotional healing began.

God cares about the whole person—which means he cares about the whole Theresa. Even though I wanted him to relieve me of my physical symptoms, God wanted me to see the underlying condition of my soul, and that condition was caused by all my unreconciled emotions and pain.

It took multiple debilitating health conditions for me to be willing to look beyond my physical issues and address my past and find the strength, courage, and insight to deal with the emotional impact and the pain they caused.

Through this healing process that began in 2016, God continues to give me a whole new perspective on my circumstances. The blessing for me is that as the emotional healing began to take place, I also began to experience physical healing. It didn't happen all at once. It's been a gradual process that I'm still uncovering.

I don't want to imply that all my physical healing resulted from my emotional healing. Only God knows that for sure. But this I do know: I didn't experience holistic health—physical, spiritual, and emotional—until *after* I was willing to address my pain and all the emotions that I had buried to avoid facing it. I wasn't ready to do that work until I found myself in a hopeless situation with my physical health.

I've also realized that what doesn't kill you can make you stronger—but only if you're willing to face the obstacle before you and learn whatever it has to teach you. I consider myself a "tough old broad." I've earned that title through years of illness and challenges. Enduring crazy sicknesses and painful experiences can make you strong, but physical strength will take you only so far. Until I strengthened my faith and dared to deal with my emotional pain, all it took was another storm, and I'd return to stuffing my emotions and adding to my growing collection of unresolved pain. But that wasn't how I wanted to live my life.

I've learned that God wants all of me, not just part of me. It wasn't until I was in a hopeless situation that I turned to him whole-heartedly, with abandon. I admitted that I wasn't only managing wounds from difficult circumstances but also self-inflicted wounds from denial, avoidance, and refusal to face my pain.

God's ways aren't my ways, and his timing isn't mine either. Looking back, I see a greater purpose in my suffering. I had to get to the depths before finally looking up at him. I had to be void of earthly solutions before surrendering to him, and I had to run out of my own answers, to trust *him* completely. I couldn't fix this, but *he* could.

Similar to when I found love only after I gave up the need to make it happen on my own, I also found physical healing after I trusted God with my emotions. And, while I've learned so much, I started to wonder if maybe there was more.

Can God use my pain for a purpose beyond myself?

What has now become clear is that I feel led to share my knowl-edge and experience about God. To share my story, all the things he's done for me and the insights he's shown me through this process.

My pain has become my purpose. I wrote this book to encour-age you through insights and provide biblical perspectives that might help you along your journey.

God isn't some distant supreme being who is uninvolved in our lives. Quite the opposite. He yearns for us to be in a relationship with him. Not because he has a huge ego that he needs us to stroke. No, he loves each of us as his children, just like you love your child or family member. He wants us to come to him, lean on him, seek him, call out to him, worship him, and love him—always and under any circumstance.

And now, my job is to tell it on the mountain, over the hills, and everywhere!

"Jesus ... said to him, 'Go home to your friends, and tell them what great things the Lord has done for you, and how he has had compassion on you' " (Mark 5:19-20 NKJV).

Part II

BIBLICAL INSIGHTS FOR HOPE AND HEALING

Chapter 4

INSIGHT 1: FIND A
FRIEND IN JESUS

I was raised in a devout Catholic home. Catholicism wasn't just a religion to us. It was our heritage and the center of our life. So, of course, we went to mass on Sundays—even when we were out of town, attending Catholic churches wherever we traveled. Some of my siblings and I went to the local Catholic school. I was there from kindergarten through eighth grade. My mom was the school secretary, and my dad was the scoutmaster for our church Boy Scout troop. As a family, we were deeply engrossed in our Catholic faith and community.

There was no shortage of religion in my childhood. I remember attending many masses—not just Sundays, but other holy days as well—not eating meat on Fridays, giving up something for Lent each year, going to confession weekly, celebrating my first Communion in first grade, and going through confirmation in eighth grade. One of my favorite memories is attending Midnight Mass on Christmas Eve. I thought no other young child was allowed to stay up until midnight on Christmas Eve. I loved the late-night ritual, and the anticipation for Santa was almost more than I could handle.

When I think about my faith, it was more about what I did than my relationship with God. My faith was about my religion—rich in tradition, ceremony, and ritual. If you asked me then about who God was, I just remember I feared him. I saw him as a God of judgment and punishment and suffering. I'm not saying this is how Catholics in general see their faith or view God, but for me, my motive for being religious was out of fear of punishment versus a desire to love God or to know God.

To me, faith was about doing or not doing—what to do and what not to do in order to avoid God's wrath or stay in his good graces. If I didn't do the right things, then it didn't matter that I had faith. Eternal punishment was ahead.

As for what I thought about God's view of me, I remember an overwhelming feeling of unworthiness and a constant judgment for my sin. I don't remember thinking much about grace, mercy, forgiveness, or love, nor that even though I was a sinner, I was always worthy of God's love.

That's pretty heavy for a kid.

Don't misunderstand me; I wholeheartedly believe there's a place for ritual, tradition, and ceremony. Ritual and tradition may support faith, but they aren't the object of faith. There's a certain level of reverence and respect that are present, but that isn't all there is to faith.

Faith involves both religion *and* a relationship. I didn't understand I was missing a faith shored up by a personal relationship with God and a desire to know him and be in constant companionship with him.

I didn't grasp that if I wanted to know God, it was my responsibility to get to know him more deeply and personally. God certainly knew me, but I didn't spend time getting to know God. I waited for priests and my catechism teachers to tell me about God, Jesus, and the Holy Spirit. I believed in God and I knew that Jesus died for our sins. But I didn't understand that I had direct access to God and that meant I could talk directly to him, personally get to know him through reading his Word, and be constantly connected to him through the Holy Spirit and prayer.

I needed to come near him so that he'd come near me (James 4:8), but since I hadn't invested in a personal relationship with God, my interest and dedication slowly disappeared as I became a teenager. By the time I went off to college, I'd abandoned my religious practices except for an occasional prayer when I found myself in need and attending mass whenever I went home. I still believed in God, but I wasn't interested in all the legalistic requirements of a God I could never satisfy. I felt like I was never going to be good enough to be worthy of his love, which seemed conditional based on my behavior, so I chose to distance myself.

John and I didn't talk about our faith much. He was Baptist, like my dad, and we both had a level of respect for each other's religious background. Once we were at college together, we'd occasionally go to church—sometimes to a Catholic mass and sometimes to a Baptist service—but neither of us was actively practicing our faith beyond that. We were typical college students focused on school, extracurricular activities, parties, and having fun—and my faith was neatly placed on a shelf.

After we settled into married life in North Carolina—John as a ground supply officer and me as a college student at UNCW and working at the local mall—my faith was still on a shelf. All was well. I didn't see the need for God beyond believing he existed, and there wasn't much happening to motivate me to grow my faith or even shore it up. It was 1983, and John was busy working. I was busy going to school, working, and planning to graduate that December, and that faith that I conveniently shelved, consisting of legalistic requirements and occasional church services, didn't prepare me for what was about to rock my world.

After John deployed to Beirut that May, I still didn't think much about my faith. Those around me at work and school didn't share my concern about something terrible happening while he was gone. It was a peacekeeping mission. I'd been told that he was more likely to be killed in a car accident in North Carolina than getting hurt while in Lebanon. Those comments weren't comforting, but I figured I must be overreacting, so I tried to stay busy and occupy my time with school and work.

But then the worst thing happened. When John was killed on October 23, 1983, I was unprepared. That faith that I had shelved wasn't strong enough to help me survive.

I found myself lost and without a savior. I didn't find comfort, direction, or answers in the rituals, traditions, and ceremonies I knew. I didn't have any personal relationship with God to lean on. I didn't know any Scriptures to shore me up in this storm since I hadn't devoted time to reading and understanding the Bible myself. I found myself as a twenty-three-year-old widow with a faith that was stuck on a shelf collecting dust, and that's not a place you want to be.

When I moved from North Carolina to Atlanta, I quickly discovered that without a consistent voice of truth deeply rooted in God's Word in my life, I was easily influenced by varying opinions that changed on a whim. I made many stumbles, left turns, and hiccups, which resulted in many regrets.

My faith was like one of the seeds Jesus referred to in the parable of the farmer who sowed seeds that fell in multiple places. I was like the seed that fell on a rocky path whose roots were shallow and withered when the sun came up (Mark 4:5-6). When tragedy struck, the roots of my faith dwindled (Mark 4:16-17). I'd done nothing to cultivate, shore up, or grow my faith. I'd done nothing to *know* God more, to have a relationship with him—so how could my faith sustain me in such a difficult time?

After I married David in 1991, we began regularly attending church. Regardless of the denomination or church we attended, I took my childhood understanding of faith—religion without relationship—with me.

All of that changed in 1999 when we moved to Arkansas and joined a local church the following year. I participated in my first adult Bible study, *Experiencing God* by Henry Blackaby,[1] in 2002. Through this study, I realized for the first time that I could have a personal relationship with God. I learned that I had a direct line to God because of the death and resurrection of Jesus (Hebrews 10:19 MSG).

When I heard that, it changed my life. My faith became personal on that day. It became more than just a ceremony, a tradition, a ritual, or a rule—it included a rich relationship directly with God. I am a daughter of God, the Father, and I can talk with God whenever about whatever. Not only with prewritten prayers, but in a real conversation with a real person. And the way I nurtured my relationship with God was to spend time getting to know him, just like I spend time getting to know my friends, family, and coworkers.

Did God want to hear about my day, that traffic jam, that dirty diaper, or that screaming baby? *Yes!*

Did he want to listen to my struggles, worries, and insecurities? *Yes!*

Was he a God of grace and mercy, patience, and goodness? *Absolutely!*

---

[1] Henry T. Blackaby, Claude V. King, *Experiencing God: Knowing and Doing the Will of God* (Nashville: LifeWay Press, 1990).

How is it that I just realized this? I have to believe that God's timing is perfect.

But I struggled with getting to know my heavenly Father, who has no beginning or ending, is all-knowing, is all-powerful, and is everlasting. From my limited human perspective, how could I relate with his omnipotent and omnipresent attributes? I had a hard time wrapping my mind around that until I realized that I could truly understand God's character by becoming better acquainted with the nature and character of Jesus.

God became man—Jesus Christ, the Son of God—perfect in every way because he was fully divine, yet relatable because he was fully human (John 1:14). Jesus faced trials and temptations of many kinds. He experienced grief, pain, anger, and joy. He lived here on Earth just like you and me. He had parents, siblings, an extended family, and a job. He celebrated good times and mourned the loss of a dear friend like the rest of us. He was tempted, tortured, and suffered, too. Jesus knows firsthand how hard this life is, which makes him the perfect role model (Hebrews 4:15 ESV).

Talk about someone who is an inspiration to all the rest of us. Understanding who Jesus is helped me better understand God's true nature and character.

After that, my faith grew into a sweet, personal relationship with God. I no longer saw him as a God of judgment but as a God of love, compassion, and mercy. I know he still is a God of judgment, but that's no longer my first image of him.

I had an insatiable desire to know him better. Reading, learning his Word, and understanding his truth were a great start, and this has become a daily spiritual practice for me—I call it my "quiet time." As our relationship has grown, I've realized I can have an ongoing honest conversation with him. He tells us to pray continually, so he's invited me to talk with him 24/7 (1 Thessalonians 5:16-18). And it's not a one-way conversation, either. I've learned to listen for God to speak to me by the Holy Spirit through the Bible, prayer, circumstances, and people. To help you design your own quiet time, I've included some resources in "Daily Quiet Time Resource Suggestions" in the appendix.

I understand now that it's up to me—not anyone else—to develop a strong faith. I have transferred the responsibility of my faith from priests and pastors to me. I have to cultivate my faith through Bible reading, prayer, and worship, participating in Bible studies, and more.

In a world where so many "truths" constantly change, it's incredibly comforting that God and his truth are unchanging. He is my true north. His Word is my instruction book for anything I encounter. His Word is alive to me, and it's remarkable how applicable it is to any of my life's challenges (Hebrews 4:12 ESV).

I've discovered a much stronger faith—a relationship where God is my father, friend, confidant, teacher, healer, and cheerleader. My ever-present help in time of need (Psalm 46:1). I've learned to look to him first when trials and troubles come my way (John 16:33).

And when I attend mass at my mom's Catholic church today, even though the ritual and ceremony haven't changed very much over the years, I realize that my heart has. When I walk into the sanctuary, God's presence and love for me come through loud and clear. The words I once spoke without meaning now flow with love and admiration and praise for my heavenly Father.

So, did the Catholic Church change? Or did I? I changed—my heart changed—and my relationship with God is the same wherever I worship him.

I am on the right road. I have a friend in Jesus.

So how about you? How do you see your relationship with God and Jesus? As friends? The hymn "What a friend we have in Jesus" has become one of my favorites. Read these lyrics by Joseph Scriven, and understand my faith journey. Then ask yourself: Do I need a friend like this?

What a Friend We Have in Jesus[2]

What a friend we have in Jesus,
all our sins and griefs to bear!
What a privilege to carry
everything to God in prayer!
O what peace we often forfeit,
O what needless pain we bear,
all because we do not carry
everything to God in prayer!

Have we trials and temptations?
Is there trouble anywhere?
We should never be discouraged;
take it to the Lord in prayer.
Can we find a friend so faithful
who will all our sorrows share?
Jesus knows our every weakness;
take it to the Lord in prayer.

Are we weak and heavy laden,
cumbered with a load of care?
Precious Savior, still our refuge—
take it to the Lord in prayer!
Do your friends despise, forsake you?
Take it to the Lord in prayer!
In his arms he'll take and shield you;
You will find a solace there.

---

[2] Scriven, Joseph. "What a Friend We Have in Jesus." Hymnary. Accessed October 2, 2023. https://hymnary.org/text/what_a_friend_we_have_in_jesus_all_our_s

Insights and Scriptures to Find a Friend in Jesus
EVERYDAY APPLICATIONS

What I learned:

1. Faith is more than religion and ritual. It includes a personal relationship with God.

2. God already knows me, but I have to get to know *him*.

3. Let Jesus be a role model for life. Jesus understands my weaknesses and temptations, since he walked this Earth and was tempted in every way. He's relatable.

4. Talk with God like he's a person. Speak to him constantly about anything. Listen for him to answer by the Holy Spirit through the Bible, prayer, circumstances, and people.

5. Cultivate my faith. No one can do it for me. Some spiritual practices include prayer, Bible reading, worship, and more.

6. God is always there for me. He is my refuge and strength in difficult circumstances.

Scriptures that led me to these insights:

• Come near to God, and he will come near to you. (James 4:8)

• Some fell on rocky places, where it did not have much soil. It sprang up quickly, because the soil was shallow. But when the sun came up, the plants were scorched, and they withered because they had no root. (Mark 4:5-6)

• Others, like seed sown on rocky places, hear the word and at once receive it with joy. But since they have no root, they last only a short time. When trouble or persecution comes because of the word, they quickly fall away. (Mark 4:16-17)

• So, friends, we can now—without hesitation—walk right up to

God, into "the Holy Place." Jesus has cleared the way by the blood of his sacrifice, acting as our priest before God. The "curtain" into God's presence is his body. (Hebrews 10:19 MSG)

- The Word became flesh and made his dwelling among us. We have seen his glory, the glory of the one and only Son, who came from the Father, full of grace and truth. (John 1:14)

- For we do not have a high priest who is unable to sympathize with our weaknesses, but one who in every respect has been tempted as we are, yet without sin. (Hebrews 4:15 ESV)

- Rejoice always, pray continually, give thanks in all circumstances; for this is God's will for you in Christ Jesus. (1 Thessalonians 5:16-18)

- For the word of God is living and active, sharper than any two-edged sword, piercing to the division of soul and of spirit, of joints and of marrow, and discerning the thoughts and intentions of the heart. (Hebrews 4:12 ESV)

- God is our refuge and strength, an ever-present help in trouble. (Psalm 46:1)

- I have told you these things, so that in me you may have peace. In this world you will have trouble. But take heart! I have overcome the world. (John 16:33)

Chapter 5

INSIGHT 2:
BELIEVE GOD

When I realized that my faith was more than just religion but also included a personal relationship with God, it finally felt real. Jesus was my new best friend. After fully embracing my newfound faith, I thought I'd "arrived." Finally, I could confidently face any of life's challenges.

Now that my faith was personal, I was committed to knowing God, having a personal relationship, and learning more about him through his Word. I pored over the Bible, participated in Bible studies, attended worship services, and spent lots of time praying. I thought my faith was on solid ground for sure.

But I didn't know that I was in for a more prolonged battle. I'd be tested through additional trials and hardships that would nearly break me again. Starting in 2008, after I began to experience difficult, prolonged health issues, I found myself getting frustrated with God. Hadn't I been through enough? Weren't death and divorce plenty for me to handle?

I began to question my relationship with God. Years of health battles were wearing me down. There were times when I was so sick I didn't *feel* God's presence. When there were no medical explanations, I started to believe God didn't *care* about me. When I cried out in the middle of so many long sleepless nights, I wondered if he even *heard* me.

I found myself in a precarious situation with my faith. I didn't question God's promises for other people or their circumstances—whether it was David, my kids, my friends, my coworkers, or anybody else. On the contrary, I believed that God's promises were true and accurate—*for everyone else.* I encouraged them with that belief as I saw each of them flourish after overcoming a difficult circumstance.

As time went on and my health battles continued for nearly a decade, I began questioning God's promises for *me.* I didn't see the results of his promises in my life as I did for others. Did he really have plans for me, plans to prosper and not harm me, plans for hope and a future (Jeremiah 29:11)? Did God really hear me (1 John 5:14 NLT)? Did he really want to heal me (Psalm 103:1, 3)?

Even though I still believed *in* God, I didn't *believe* God or his Word for *me.* I let my circumstances define my outlook. My ongoing health challenges were taking their toll. Once I'd get over one thing, something else would crop up, and I'd have another battle on my hands. I wondered if I was again in a place where I was like that seed that fell on a rocky place (Mark 4:16-17). Rattled when tragedy struck. I was doing many things to cultivate my faith—Bible study, prayer, and worship. What was I missing?

Once again, I found myself in the middle of a faith crisis.

One thing was apparent even at my lowest point, even when I wondered if God cared about me. I didn't have anywhere else to turn. I had reached *my* limits. I wasn't getting any answers or relief for my health problems from the medical community, and I knew I couldn't heal myself because I'd been trying to do that for years.

I'd already lived without leaning on God for many years, and that hadn't worked. So, even though I doubted his promises for me, I continued to do what I knew how to do. I prayed, dug deeper into his Word, cried, and privately unloaded my burdens on him just as his Word commands (Matthew 11:28). Like King David cried out in so many Psalms, I did the same.

Since the Bible is like my life's instruction book, I searched for any hint or answer for this long health battle—for any indication of healing. I spent lots of time in the Gospels reading about the miracles of Jesus—specifically when he healed people. I yearned for that healing, too—to be free from the ongoing physical pain and sickness—to be a healthy Theresa and no longer be a sick Theresa.

As only God does, in his way and his time, I had another aha moment—found it right there in the text:

"According to your faith let it be done to you" (Matthew 9:29). And, " 'take heart daughter,' he said, 'your faith has healed you' " (Matthew 9:22).

Those verses had one thing in common—the people in them believed God and what he said, *before* their healing occurred, while they were still suffering. They *believed* God—they didn't just believe *in* him.

After pondering and praying about those verses, I realized that I was waiting for healing to happen *first* before truly believing God's word for myself. I wanted proof before I fully believed him. Dang, I was no different from the Israelites and the Pharisees. They demanded to see signs and miracles before they believed God, and I was doing the same thing (Matthew 12:38 NLT).

Another verse gave me pause in the Gospel of Matthew. While Jesus was in his hometown, many questioned who he was. Jesus refused to perform miracles there because they showed a lack of faith (Matthew 13:58). Well, that stopped me in my tracks. It says right there he didn't perform any miracles because they lacked faith. They didn't *believe* Jesus and what he was saying.

I was doing the same thing. How could I expect God to heal me if I didn't even believe what his Word says?

It was time to get my act together and *choose* to believe regardless of my healing.

This *is not* a guarantee for healing. Only God knows when you or I will be healed—could be this side of heaven, or not. But if I don't believe God's promises for me, I've removed myself from his work in my life. I've shut the door before God has a chance to open it.

It's easy to believe God's Word when life is going well, when you feel good and all is right in your world. Remaining faithful is challenging when the storms return and your boat rocks again. The faith I'd so carefully cultivated was tested for several years, but that's when believing God and his promises is needed *most*. It's remaining certain in uncertain times in uncertain situations. It means having faith that's *all in*, regardless of your circumstances.

Is that easy? Nope. It's a decision. You have a choice. Here are some of the questions I wrestled with:

- Do I believe God and what He says in his Word, no matter my circumstances?

- Or do I *believe in him* but doubt what he says, particularly when life deals me a tough hand?

- Do I hedge my bets to wait and see the miracle before I profess my faith in God?

Here is what I've learned about faith. Our consistent faith in God, in who he is, and what he says he can do, can help us stand in the middle of the storms—to believe God, no matter our circumstances.

- To have faith and hope even when it looks like a hopeless situation (Hebrews 11:1).

- To believe his Word even when your world is upside down (Proverbs 30:5).

- To know he is with you and will never forsake you (Deuteronomy 31:8).

- To be assured that all things are possible with God, regardless of your circumstances (Matthew 19:26).

- To know that in all things, he is always at work for our good (Romans 8:28).

That is a steadfast faith. And it's a decision.

It's cultivated by spending deep personal time with God and by *knowing* his Word. That means consistently reading and studying it, writing down verses that resonate, and committing meaningful verses to memory. I like keeping a Scripture journal, so I can quickly remind myself of those verses that lift me, give me hope, and reassure me of God's presence in my life.

Sometimes our faith can waver, and that's okay. Jesus talks about it in the Gospel of Mark when a man is seeking healing for his mute son. The man asks *if* Jesus can take pity on them and help his son. Jesus quickly reassures the father that anything is possible if a person believes. The man immediately proclaims his belief and asks Jesus to help him with his unbelief, all before Jesus heals the boy (Mark 9:23-24 NLT).

I wish I could say that I have rock-solid faith every day, hour, and minute. I wish I could say that my faith is *always* unfaltering. But I'm still human. I still have those knee-jerk reactions when something comes along to rock my boat. I sometimes feel doubt overcome me, but this story shows us what to do when we find ourselves in doubt. When your faith feels shaky, ask God to help you with your unbelief.

I've learned that it's okay to tell God my fears, disappointment, frustrations, and struggles. He already knows them anyway, so I don't have to get my act together before I pray. On the contrary, I can go to God with all my uncertainty and frustrations and lay it all out for him to hear.

I'm comforted when I read many of the Psalms written by King David, when he laments over a particular situation or difficulty with cries of anguish and sorrow. For example, David asks God how long God will forget him (Psalm 13:1) and how long David's enemies will triumph over him (Psalm 13:2).

In the same Psalm, after spilling his guts to the Lord, King David pledges his trust in God and sings his praises. He believed that God was his refuge and sovereign over everything, even in difficult circumstances.

These Scriptures show us that we can be vulnerable to God and let him know our struggles and, at the same time, continue to believe and trust God, knowing he is ultimately in control. Through these Psalms, I realized that I could let it all out with God, and in the end, still trust that he is in control and praise him.

When I'm overcome with doubt, or when new health challenges or unexpected circumstances arrive, I like to do something I call "getting my mind right." This is my code phrase to my husband, David. He knows when I say that, I need a few hours to work things out in my heart and mind with the Lord.

Where quiet time is a daily practice, getting my mind right happens on a case-by-case basis. It's a time when I can be away from others and react however I need to when a situation calls for some extra time to visit with God—and maybe even scream, yell, or cry—about whatever is going on in my life.

I've learned that mindset matters. I find it helpful to go for a long drive alone—preferably somewhere around the Buffalo National River, just an hour from our house in the Ozark Mountains, and the scenery is beautiful. I see God's hand in the beauty of my surroundings, which makes me feel even closer to him.

During that time, I spend a few hours letting it all out—by praying, crying, lamenting, searching, and talking with the Lord. God sweetly and gently reminds me of many of his promises by flooding my mind with his Word. At just the right moment I am reminded of Scriptures encouraging me not to be afraid and to know God is with me (Joshua 1:9), and that he'll strengthen me and help me (Isaiah 41:10).

Little by little, I am reassured that God's already got this new challenge in his control. He knows about it, and he already has a solution. He's working it all out for my good. My job is to *believe him* and wait expectantly for him to work his plan.

By the time I'm done with my long drive letting out my struggles with the Lord, he blesses me with renewed strength, perseverance, and hope (1 Peter 5:10).

Insights and Scriptures to Believe God
EVERYDAY APPLICATIONS

What I learned:

1. Believing God is a decision. It's more than believing *in* God. It means that I believe what he says in his Word and his promises for me, regardless of my circumstances.

2. Believe God *before* seeing signs and miracles. Believe God *before* seeing proof of my prayers answered.

3. Read the Bible and know Scripture before I need it in a difficult situation. Make reading the Bible an ongoing spiritual discipline *now*. When difficult circumstances come my way, I can lean on Scripture I've already read for reassurance during tough times.

4. Create a Scripture journal. Fill it with meaningful Bible verses, and refer to it whenever I need encouragement or reassurance. Create a digital version so I can quickly access it whenever and wherever needed.

5. When my faith wavers, take it to God. Ask him to help me with any disbelief.

6. Be vulnerable with God and share all frustrations, doubts, and concerns. Be honest, but like King David in Psalms, know that God is sovereign over all things and trust him with my circumstances.

Scriptures that led me to these insights:

- "For I know the plans I have for you," declares the Lord, "plans to prosper you and not to harm you, plans to give you hope and a future." (Jeremiah 29:11)

- And we are confident that he hears us whenever we ask for anything that pleases him. (1 John 5:14 NLT)

- Praise the Lord, my soul; all my inmost being, praise his holy name ... who forgives all your sins and heals all your diseases. (Psalm 103:1, 3)

- Others, like seed sown on rocky places, hear the word and at once receive it with joy. But since they have no root, they last only a short time. When trouble or persecution comes because of the word, they quickly fall away. (Mark 4:16-17)

- Come to me, all you who are weary and burdened, and I will give you rest. (Matthew 11:28)

- According to your faith let it be done to you. (Matthew 9:29)

- "Take heart, daughter," he said, "your faith has healed you." (Matthew 9:22)

- One day some teachers of religious law and Pharisees came to Jesus and said, "Teacher, we want you to show us a miraculous sign to prove your authority." (Matthew 12:38 NLT)

- And he did not do many miracles there because of their lack of faith. (Matthew 13:58)

- Now faith is confidence in what we hope for and assurance about what we do not see. (Hebrews 11:1)

- Every word of God proves true; he is a shield to those who take refuge in him. (Proverbs 30:5 ESV)

- The LORD himself goes before you and will be with you; he will never leave you nor forsake you. Do not be afraid; do not be discouraged. (Deuteronomy 31:8)

- Jesus looked at them and said, "With man this is impossible, but with God all things are possible." (Matthew 19:26)

- And we know that in all things God works for the good of those who love him, who have been called according to his purpose. (Romans 8:28)

- "What do you mean, 'If I can'?" Jesus asked. "Anything is possible if a person believes." The father instantly cried out, "I do believe, but help me overcome my unbelief!" (Mark 9:23-24 NLT)

- How long, Lord? Will you forget me forever? How long will you hide your face from me? (Psalm 13:1)

- How long must I wrestle with my thoughts and day after day have sorrow in my heart? How long will my enemy triumph over me? (Psalm 13:2)

- Have I not commanded you? Be strong and courageous. Do not be afraid; do not be discouraged, for the Lord your God will be with you wherever you go. (Joshua 1:9)

- So do not fear, for I am with you; do not be dismayed, for I am your God. I will strengthen you and help you; I will uphold you with my righteous right hand. (Isaiah 41:10)

- And the God of all grace, who called you to his eternal glory in Christ, after you have suffered a little while, will himself restore you and make you strong, firm and steadfast. (1 Peter 5:10)

Chapter 6

INSIGHT 3: KNOW THE TRUE ENEMY

Although my faith was maturing with new spiritual insights, my ongoing physical challenges continued, and I wavered in my faith once again. Over time, I began to think God was punishing me for something done in my past, some sin that I'd committed. And, if a past sin wasn't the reason, I wondered if God was just picking on me?

That kind of thinking is normal—just read the book of Job about a man who endured a long season of pain and suffering. His friends spent nearly forty-one chapters telling him that it was something he did or didn't do that brought about his calamity and physical condition.

We know that wasn't the case with Job. Before undergoing his challenges, God deemed Job blameless and upright, a man who feared God and turned away from evil (Job 1:8). And yet Job underwent an incredibly long season of suffering and loss. His goodness didn't prevent his situation. Even though Job's livestock and servants were destroyed, and his home collapsed and killed his children, Job's initial reaction was to bow down and worship God rather than blame God (Job 1:20,22). He understood that his faith in God didn't protect him from anything bad ever happening (Job 2:10).

However, as Job's trials worsened, Job began to question God. He asked God, "Why did I not perish at birth, and die as I came from the womb?" (Job 3:11). And, "Why let people go on living in misery… they wait for death, but it never comes (Job 3:21-22 GNT). He even got dangerously close to suggesting that God didn't care by asking, "Why have you made me your target? Have I become a burden to you?" (Job 7:20).

Those questions resonated with me. Whenever I overcame a challenge, in the back of my mind, I was always waiting for the next challenge to show up, for the next battle. I convinced myself that God loved everyone except me, that his promises were meant for everyone else, and that he decided that my destiny in this life on earth was to suffer. Although I knew I wasn't exempt from trouble in my life (John 16:33), it sure felt like I had more than my share.

Didn't it matter that I'd already undergone a tragic death in my youth? Wasn't that enough?

I was trying to live a faithful life devoting my life to David and my kids. Like Job, I began asking God questions.

Why are you allowing this to happen to me? Why do you hate me? Why is this going on for so long? What have I done to deserve this?

I've come to understand that God welcomes our questions when we're doubting or in despair. He wants us to bring those questions to him in prayer to wrestle and process with him, take refuge in him, and ask for his wisdom for our circumstances. King David asked God many questions in his distress while also professing his trust in God (Psalm 13:1-2, 5-6).

Where I strayed was when I failed to lean on God's Word to remind me of his character and his love for me before I decided he had it in for me. God's love is constant, and he sees my suffering and anguish (Psalm 31:7 GNT). He is sovereign over all things, and his ways are not always our ways (Isaiah 55:8-9). He is always at work for my good even when I don't see it (Romans 8:28). Rather than taking those truths to heart, once again I began to doubt God's faithfulness and love for me.

One day, I was telling David how I felt like I was being punished by God, that God didn't care about me, and David said, "Theresa, you have an enemy, but it's not God!"

It stopped me in my tracks and shifted my view on my situation. In all of my suffering, I hadn't considered the role of Satan in any of this. Satan had discovered my weakness, a chink in my armor that caused me to doubt my faith in God, doubt that he loved me, doubt that he had plans to prosper me and not to harm me (Jeremiah 29:11). Satan knew I had a breaking point. Isn't that what Satan did to Eve right from the start—to plant some seeds of doubt in her? In Genesis, he said, "Did God really say … ?" (Genesis 3:1), causing Eve to question what she knew to be true.

Until David's comment, I was misdirected in thinking about who my enemy really was. I realized then that the enemy was causing me to doubt God's love for me—subtly, yet constantly.

I can only imagine how heartbroken God was. Hearing how I misjudged him, deciding that he was attacking me—that *he* was my enemy, while the real enemy, Satan, was sitting back, satisfied that his schemes were working to change my faith in God from a firm belief to doubt and disbelief. Isn't it interesting that this happened after I really started digging deep in my faith? After I was trying to develop a close relationship with God? I believe Satan wanted nothing more than to sever that relationship, and he'd do anything to accomplish that.

You see, we really do have an enemy. Satan is real. Not some fictitious character. The devil is prominent throughout the Bible. He started wreaking havoc from the get-go. The enemy showed up and started telling lies in the garden of Eden. Satan twisted God's words, casting doubt, by telling Adam and Eve they wouldn't die if they ate from the tree of the knowledge of good and evil like God warned. He also tempted them by saying they could be like God without consequences (Genesis 3:4-5). Satan even tried to tempt Jesus to turn stone into bread when he was hungry after fasting in the desert for forty days and nights (Matthew 4:2-3).

And the enemy has been showing up ever since, continuing to tell lies, cast doubt, and deceive. Let's face it: Satan wants to destroy each of us (John 10:10), and he'll do it any way he can. He roams around like a roaring lion, looking for anyone to devour (1 Peter 5:8), but he's not very creative. He just looks for our weaknesses, then he attempts to destroy us with them.

The way I see it, Satan saw my newfound enthusiasm to know God and his Word, figured out where I might have the most significant distraction, and decided that would be his battleground. As health challenges overcame me, Satan started bombarding me with lies that God was my enemy. Since I was in such pain and felt horrible, I even found it hard to strengthen myself by reading the Bible or praying. I grew weak in my faith, which gave Satan more reason to pour on the gas.

Although I'd have occasional reprieves from my struggles and focus more on strengthening my faith, when another round of challenges came my way I'd be right back in the battle. In hindsight, I can see that I was an easy mark.

There was no reprieve from Satan's whispers of doubt and fear. Attacks like, "this pain and illness are never going to end," "God really doesn't care about you," and "you don't deserve healing" were constantly bombarding my thoughts. The reality was that Satan was slowly but surely breaking me.

David wasn't done with his observations, and what he said next was even more impactful. He reminded me that I wasn't alone in my battle; this was God's battle to fight (2 Chronicles 20:15). That was another pivotal point for me because I realized God was in charge, and he'd lead the way. I was on his team, and I could use his powerful spiritual weapons to fight my battles (2 Corinthians 10:4 GNT).

All along I was thinking my battle was with God when it had

been with Satan. I needed to redirect my focus. I knew that even though the physical hardship may continue, I wanted to be ready to fight my real enemy when he attacked me again.

Satan is roaming around, ready to pounce at any time. To attack. To cause doubt. To whisper lies in the hopes that we'll believe him and not God. I don't know about you, but I do *not* want to fall prey to his sneakiness. We have an enemy and the *real* enemy isn't people, places, or circumstances—and especially *not* God (Ephesians 6:12).

I want to take a stand. I want to be prepared, and I want you to be, too. But how do we fight? What can we do to prepare for our battles? Here are four strategies that I've found useful:

First, proactively prepare for the battle daily.

The Bible says to put on the full armor of God so we can take a stand against the enemy (Ephesians 6:13). This Scripture is not a suggestion. It doesn't say that you *might* want to do this or that it *could* help you take a stand. It's straightforward. It says to *put on*. Recognize you're in a battle, look at your circumstances knowing that Satan may be involved, and be prepared and fight him.

Second, make sure you have the right weapons for your battle.

What are those? Start with the Bible (Ephesians 6:17). Commit to knowing what it says. The only way to do that is to read the Bible, *and* study it consistently. Studying is different from reading. It involves understanding it more deeply.

I have a Life Application Study Bible, which includes footnotes, illustrations, maps, and diagrams to help me further understand the Scripture I'm reading. I also use online Bible resources like BibleRef (https://www.bibleref.com) whenever I need clarification of verses. As I take the time to learn, I can answer questions like, "What does this verse say?" "What does it mean?" and "How can this change me?" The result is that God's Word becomes a part of me, and it affects me—my thoughts, attitudes, and behaviors.

Third, memorize key Bible verses.

Consider when Jesus was led into the desert for forty days, and Satan tempted him. Do you know how he fought the enemy? He spoke the very Word of God from memory (Luke 4:4, 8, 12). Did Jesus pull out his Bible app and look up verses? Nope, he quoted them from memory. Three times Satan tempted Jesus, and three times Jesus quoted Scriptures to fend off Satan's attacks.

Do you know what happened when Jesus did this? After Satan finished tempting Jesus with his lies to no avail, the enemy left (Luke 4:13). This tactic looked like a great approach for me to implement. I wanted to recall verses instead of searching through my Bible while in the heat of the battle.

When I realized that memorizing Scripture was a way to fight these attacks, I had a new sense of urgency to prepare myself. I like to call it "carb up." I used to run 5K and 10K races. The night before a race, I'd always eat a high carbohydrate meal to build up my energy and help my performance the day of the race. Runners refer to that process as "carbing up," and I see memorizing Scriptures as serving a similar purpose.

I've memorized various Bible verses to serve different functions in battle—to encourage me to keep fighting, reassure me that God is always with me, or comfort and strengthen me in my struggles. I've included a reference to some of those Scriptures in "Ten Scriptures to Fight the Enemy" in the appendix.

If memorizing doesn't come easily to you, then I get that. I thought the same thing. But nothing else was working in my battles, so I figured it out. I don't have all of them memorized perfectly. Sometimes I know a particular Scripture by heart but I have a hard time remembering the specific book and verse of the Bible. Other times, I know the sentiment of the verse, even if I don't have the exact wording. It still works for me. Jesus said, "It is written," then he would fight Satan with a Scripture. He didn't tell Satan which book the Scripture was found in—Satan already knew. The main point is to equip yourself with some key Bible verses and make the effort to memorize some. If I can do it, you can too. To help you, I've included a few Scripture memorization suggestions in "Scripture Memorization Techniques" in the appendix.

Being prepared ahead of the battle is ideal, but maybe you're already in the struggle like I was. Even though I was in the battle well before I realized that Scripture memorization was necessary, it wasn't too late for me to get started. It's never too late. I continue to make it a lifelong discipline. Unfortunately, our battles will continue this side of heaven, so this needs to become a long-term discipline.

Fourth, place reminders everywhere.

I wrote Bible verses on note cards and Post-it notes, and I hung them wherever I'd see them. There were Scriptures in the kitchen, in my bathroom, in my car, and at my desk. God's reassuring Word that I wasn't alone was visible all around me, so whenever Satan whispered doubt and fear, I immediately started my counterattack by praying and even speaking those Scriptures aloud.

When I did that, the fear subsided and the doubt dissipated, and I found strength to keep on keeping on. Over time, those Scriptures were etched in my mind and on my heart. Hear me in this: there is power in the spoken Word of God, and Jesus' example in the desert is proof. If he fought off Satan this way and succeeded, then by golly, I'm going to do this, too.

And timing matters, doesn't it? When soldiers go into battle, they don't put on their combat gear *after* they're in the fight. They put it on *before*. Just like when a runner runs a race, she loads up with proper nutrients and energy *before* the race begins, not once it starts.

Similarly, what works best in the spiritual realm is reading, studying, and memorizing Bible verses *before* the battle begins. That's how we should prepare for our day-to-day battles, too. Be proactive. Just like athletes have physical disciplines to be at their best for competition, let's develop some spiritual disciplines to prepare for our battles.

Now when the battle begins, I find that I'm quicker to detect the enemy's schemes and a whole lot faster to fight back, just like Jesus did in the desert. I can recall several Scriptures from memory that have equipped me to fight the fight, persevere, and know God is at work for my good.

Our minds are a battleground for Satan's attacks. The enemy thrives on filling our minds with lots of lies. Before we know it, our thoughts are spiraling out of control. Satan *still* likes to feed me with lies, but God's Word says that he didn't give us a spirit of fear or cowardice, but of power, love, and self-control (2 Timothy 1:7 ESV).

So, the sooner we realize that fear isn't from God and that it's the enemy's lies that we're hearing, the better. Once we recognize that, it's our responsibility to stop those lies in their tracks and take them captive (2 Corinthians 10:5). Awareness comes first, and actively shutting down those thoughts and reminding yourself of the truth in God's Word comes next. They work hand in hand. The Bible says when we resist the devil, he'll flee. So shut him down (James 4:7).

God has a plan, and so does Satan. Just as God has plans to prosper us and not harm us, Satan's plans are to destroy us.

You may be in a battle as you're reading this (I think we're always in a fight, to a certain degree, regardless of our life circumstances), and you may be tired of fighting. When you're exhausted, discouraged, and ready to give up, remember that you're not alone in your battle. God is for you. He is on your team, *and* he'll never abandon you. He wants to help you through this. He wants to fight for you. He wants you to be victorious.

Insights and Scriptures to Know the True Enemy
EVERYDAY APPLICATIONS

What I learned:

1. I have an enemy, and it's not God.

2. My enemy is Satan. He exists and is not some fictitious character. He's been at work from the beginning of time, and he wants to destroy me.

3. The battle is not mine to fight alone. It's God's battle, and I'm on his team. I can use his powerful spiritual weapons to fight the enemy.

4. Proactively prepare to recognize the enemy and stand against Satan's attacks.

5. Don't passively read the Bible. Study it. Understand what it means and how it can change me.

6. Memorize Scripture, so I can fight against the enemy as Jesus did in the desert.

7. Place Bible verses that are helpful in my battle in prominent places where I see them and are reminded.

8. Satan often attacks my thoughts and cultivates doubt and fear with his lies. Be aware of Satan's lies and take thoughts of doubt and fear captive.

9. Be aware of the enemy's lies and actively shut them down with God's truth.

Scriptures that led me to these insights:

• Then the Lord said to Satan, "Have you considered my servant Job? There is no one on earth like him; he is blameless and upright, a man who fears God and shuns evil." (Job 1:8)

79

- At this, Job got up and tore his robe and shaved his head. Then he fell to the ground in worship. ... In all this, Job did not sin by charging God with wrongdoing. (Job 1:20, 22)

- He replied, "You are talking like a foolish woman. Shall we accept good from God, and not trouble?" (Job 2:10)

- "Why did I not perish at birth, and die as I came from the womb?" (Job 3:11)

- Why let people go on living in misery? ... They wait for death, but it never comes. (Job 3:21-22 GNT)

- "If I have sinned, what have I done to you, you who see everything we do? Why have you made me your target? Have I become a burden to you?" (Job 7:20)

- "I have said these things to you, that in me you may have peace. In the world you will have tribulation. But take heart; I have overcome the world." (John 16:33)

- How long, LORD? Will you forget me forever? How long will you hide your face from me? How long must I wrestle with my thoughts and day after day have sorrow in my heart? How long will my enemy triumph over me? ... But I trust in your unfailing love; my heart rejoices in your salvation. I will sing the Lord's praise, for he has been good to me. (Psalm 13:1-2,5-6)

- I will be glad and rejoice in your love, for you saw my affliction and knew the anguish of my soul. (Psalm 31:7 GNT)

- "For my thoughts are not your thoughts, neither are your ways my ways," declares the Lord. "As the heavens are higher than the earth, so are my ways higher than your ways and my thoughts than your thoughts. (Isaiah 55:8-9)

- And we know that in all things God works for the good of those who love him, who have been called according to his purpose. (Romans 8:28)

- "For I know the plans I have for you," declares the Lord, "plans to prosper you and not to harm you, plans to give you hope and a future." (Jeremiah 29:11)

- Now the serpent was more crafty than any of the wild animals the Lord had made. He said, "Did God really say, 'You must not eat from any tree in the garden.' " (Genesis 3:1)

- "You will not certainly die," the serpent said to the woman. "For God knows that when you eat from it your eyes will be opened, and you will be like God, knowing good and evil." (Genesis 3:4-5)

- After fasting forty days and forty nights, he was hungry. The tempter came to him and said, "If you are the Son of God, tell these stones to become bread." (Matthew 4:2-3)

- The thief comes only to steal and kill and destroy; I have come that they may have life, and have it to the full. (John 10:10)

- Be alert and of sober mind. Your enemy the devil prowls around like a roaring lion looking for someone to devour. (1 Peter 5:8)

- Do not be afraid or discouraged because of this vast army. For the battle is not yours, but God's. (2 Chronicles 20:15)

- The weapons we use in our fight are not the world's weapons but God's powerful weapons, which we use to destroy strongholds. (2 Corinthians 10:4 GNT)

- For our struggle is not against flesh and blood, but against the rulers, against the authorities, against the powers of this dark world and against the spiritual forces of evil in the heavenly realms. (Ephesians 6:12)

- Therefore put on the full armor of God, so that when the day of evil comes, you may be able to stand your ground, and after you have done everything, to stand. (Ephesians 6:13)

- Take the helmet of salvation and the sword of the Spirit, which is the word of God. (Ephesians 6:17)

- Jesus answered, "It is written: 'Man shall not live on bread alone.' " (Luke 4:4)

- Jesus answered, "It is written: 'Worship the Lord your God and serve Him only.' " (Luke 4:8)

- Jesus answered, "It is said: 'Do not put the Lord your God to the test.' " (Luke 4:12)

- When the devil had finished all this tempting, he left him until an opportune time. (Luke 4:13)

- For God gave us a spirit not of fear but of power and love and self-control. (2 Timothy 1:7 ESV)

- We demolish arguments and every pretension that sets itself up against the knowledge of God, and we take captive every thought to make it obedient to Christ. (2 Corinthians 10:5)

- Resist the devil, and he will flee. (James 4:7)

- But he said to me, "My grace is sufficient for you, for my power is made perfect in weakness." (2 Corinthians 12:9)

Chapter 7

INSIGHT 4: TRUST GOD

I've realized there are many phases to our spiritual journey. It's a life-long process, more like a marathon than a sprint. I've progressed from a faith that was merely about religion and ritual to a faith that includes a deep relationship with God. I moved from believing in God to believing God—to believe his plans and promises for me. Learning to trust God was the next step on my spiritual path.

Even though I *believed God*, did I trust him—regardless of my circumstances? Was I surrendered to him? Did I look only to him? Or was I still trying to be in control and lean on my limited understanding of my situation? My next challenge showed me that believing God and trusting him are different things.

My most difficult health challenge began in late summer 2016 before Tyler's senior year of high school. He was playing on a traveling basketball team in a competitive summer league for students interested in playing at the college level. The team played in several tournaments across the US where college coaches often attended to scout recruits. Since Tyler had aspirations of playing college basketball, we'd travel any distance to help him. By the end of that summer, we'd driven from Arkansas to Myrtle Beach to Dallas to Las Vegas and back to Arkansas— nearly 5,000 miles—in thirty days. It was exhilarating and stressful.

Once we returned home, my stomach issues returned. It felt like someone was punching me in the gut, I was nauseated all the time, and my weight started dropping.

At first, I chalked up my nausea to eating fast food for an entire month. My body has never reacted well to lots of overly processed food, and I figured eating out three meals a day for a month would make anyone with a sensitive stomach slightly off. But, as time went on, it didn't matter what I ate, constant nausea plagued me, and it dragged on for months.

This was my third time in seven years to deal with severe stomach issues, so I did what I knew how to do. First, I went to my medical doctors, who didn't see anything alarming after lots of tests. Second, I returned to my naturopathic doctors. They had always been successful in pinpointing some food sensitivity or giving me a supplement to help, but even after I followed all the recommendations, the constant nausea continued. I was eating as best I could at the time, but the weight continued to drop, and I felt horrible 24/7.

I was determined to keep life as normal as possible for my family and still handle my responsibilities at home and work as best I could. I wanted Tyler's senior year to be a positive memory, so I kept following the advice of my doctors, even when it wasn't working.

That fall, I shared my situation with my dear friend Brandi. I told her how I felt helpless and weary from my years-long health battle.

Brandi offered me sweet empathy and compassion. She often

said, "God just wants to be your shepherd," and "Theresa, you just need to be his sheep."

I was intrigued by her comments. I'd read many references about sheep and shepherds in the Bible over the years, including Psalm 23. This well-known passage was read during the memorial service for John, but I had never explored the sheep-shepherd concept to fully understand how it related to me personally.

When I asked Brandi to explain her comments, she shared the book *A Shepherd Looks at Psalm 23*[1] by Phillip Keller. She'd had it for a very long time and gave me her copy. It looked like an antique with its yellowed pages, but rather than seeing it as some old, outdated book, I felt like it might have some age-old wisdom and perspective.

It's written from the viewpoint of a shepherd providing the constant care that sheep require. Keller has experience in this profession and provides helpful perspectives as he explains each verse in detail.

King David, who was a shepherd before becoming a king, knew firsthand sheep's nature and their complete dependence on him for their care. But King David also saw himself like a sheep in constant need of God's care, and when he wrote Psalm 23, he referred to God as his shepherd.

Keller explains that sheep are dependent, helpless, and fearful. They're also stubborn. He writes that they're the neediest livestock of all and require constant care by the shepherd to have a healthy, flourishing life. Keller observes from his own flock that since sheep are totally helpless, they quickly follow him. It's like they instinctively sense that he knows best.

He goes on to say that a good shepherd cares for his sheep because that's part of the job *and* because he loves them. Sheep matter to the shepherd, and it's a 24/7 job to ensure that the sheep have a life free from fear, hunger, disease, and danger. Keller

---

[1] W. Phillip Keller, *A Shepherd Looks at Psalm 23* (Grand Rapids: Zondervan, 1970).

explains that the quality of a sheep's life depends entirely on the quality of the shepherd's care.

We're so much like sheep and in need of a shepherd, and God wants us to embrace our dependency so he can care for us (Ezekiel 34:11-12). I can't say that I'd ever thought of myself as a sheep before, but the more I read and studied Keller's book, the more I understood the comparison, and the more I could see myself.

I often act independently of God, thinking I know what's best. The idea of surrender isn't natural to me. My nature is to take charge—be self-sufficient, pull myself up by my bootstraps. I used to think it was biblical that God helps those who help themselves, but come to find out that's not even in the Bible.

I also could see so many similarities between the shepherd and God. God is constantly watching over me. He knows everything about me. He knows what exactly is making me sick and why (Isaiah 53:6).

God wants me to flourish, so if I want to look to God as my shepherd, I have to be more like a sheep. I have to surrender my care to him. I have to trust him with my life, depend on him, and follow him.

My mother-in-law, Joey, has a beautiful saying that she shared with me many years ago: "Trust is my only part." I'm not sure if she made that up or heard it from someone else, but that succinctly states what God wants for our relationship with him.

So here I was facing another turning point in my faith experience. I already had a relationship with God. I had chosen to believe him, his Word, and the promises he makes to us in Scripture. This led to new questions. Would I admit that I'm a sheep and trust that God knows best? Would I look to him for my constant care?

I wasn't ready to surrender, yet. Not completely.

Times of desperation can drive us to a deeper place in our faith—to a place where we've looked everywhere else, and all we have left is our shepherd. But I had a little more of my journey to go before I could see that.

My illness continued into 2017, with no medical solutions. I figured it was time to go outside the local medical community and seek the best expertise I could find. I had some family members and friends who had remarkable success at the Mayo Clinic in Rochester, Minnesota. Going to Mayo felt like going to Mecca. Surely they'd know what was going on with me. David was distressed about my health. He'd been watching me practically disappear before his eyes, so he was on board.

The timing was critical. We were at the height of Tyler's high school basketball season when we made this decision. I didn't want to miss any of his games or other senior year activities, so we set our eyes on trying to make an appointment during his spring break while he was on his senior trip with some friends.

When we called Mayo, there weren't any appointments available during that time. However, they encouraged us to keep calling.

It was time to turn on the prayers big time.

I felt strongly about sending an email to more than 100 family members, friends, and coworkers asking for specific prayers. God gave me courage to write and explain my health battle in detail and include specific Bible verses and wisdom that he was putting on my heart. This was so unlike me. Remember, I keep things to myself. I stuff my issues.

The response to my email was overwhelming. People prayed and wanted me to heal. I found my "prayer warriors" who were willing to go on this challenging experience with me.

Every week or two, I'd send an update on my progress and ask for additional prayers. I included new Scripture and thoughts that God had put on my heart. I wanted to make the updates as much about God as about my own needs. And, every week, I'd receive more encouragement and prayers. It seemed like God, my shepherd, was definitely in support of this.

Our prayers were answered. I got an appointment to meet with a leading gastroenterologist during Tyler's spring break week. This began what I hoped would be a discovery and diagnosis. Healing was on the way. Finally, my shepherd was leading me on the right path to a healthy life.

After seeing Tyler off on his trip, David and I loaded up our car and headed to Rochester. The weather cooperated and we safely arrived. We were nervous but hopeful, and I continued to receive encouraging emails and texts from my prayer warriors.

Mayo did not disappoint. It is an excellent medical facility. They treat their patients with the utmost care and concern. As I walked the halls to my appointments, I felt a deep sense of God's presence. All the doctors and other staff had a heart of compassion, service, and love for the patients and their families there.

I met with my lead doctor. Before I could say anything, he outlined my entire medical history and asked several detailed questions. It was obvious he had spent time getting to know my case before I ever walked in the door.

He recommended various tests and procedures. He also suggested that I meet with a doctor in the Department of Psychiatry and Psychology since stress can factor in gastro issues. I was taken off guard because I wasn't anticipating that Mayo would consider an emotional aspect of this illness. It was one thing for a friend to bring it up, but to have the experts also draw attention to the possibility was a new surprise, but I was open to whatever he recommended. I even asked for an appointment with a gynecologist since I was having some unrelated hormonal issues. Might as well take advantage of the fact that I was surrounded by every kind of medical expertise.

Within a few minutes, I was given a detailed schedule for the remainder of the week. I had appointments for tests, blood work, and procedures along with a final recap appointment at the end of the week with my lead doctor. In a typical medical environment, it would've taken months to schedule what was going to take place in four days—medical Mecca.

As I reviewed my schedule, I saw that they weren't able to make an appointment with a psychologist. I was disappointed, but the staff reassured me and recommended that I continue to check with that department daily to see if their schedule had freed up.

Yes, Mayo was where I was going to get healed! My shepherd was taking care of me!

The days were full, and many tests were grueling—lots of fasting, swallowing cameras, another endoscopy, food sensitivity tests, and more. I felt poked and prodded from all ends, but I also felt like I was where I was supposed to be and remained hopeful.

I checked in with the Department of Psychiatry and Psychology regularly. We were nearing the end of the week and still had no success. As David often does, he started to befriend the people at that office telling them more about my situation. Lo and behold, on the last day, an appointment became available with the department chairman, who was also a psychiatrist.

Yes, God was in this.

Our appointment was brief with the psychiatrist. I quickly explained my situation with my illness. I also told him I had severe sleep issues. The stomach pain and nausea kept me awake at night. We talked about how I was a little stressed with Tyler's senior year and a bit of a worrier. These seemed to be normal concerns of most (if not all) of the other moms I knew—not something that I needed medication for or something that would cause this level of physical distress.

At the end of my brief appointment, he told me that stress and worry could wreak havoc on the digestive system. I listened but figured there must be additional physical things that were making me sick. He prescribed some medication that would help with sleep and stress, and I was on my way.

The final appointment with the lead doctor was upon us. Surely they had found the real issue. Surely there was something physically wrong with me. Surely the camera endoscopy, blood work, or any of the other procedures I'd endured showed a problem.

There we sat face-to-face with my lead doctor for the final findings, and the doctor said that physically everything looked great.

Since everything came back normal, he recommended that I discontinue abstaining from any food going forward (gluten, dairy, etc.)—get back to eating gluten, dairy, sugar, and all the other things I had given up in an attempt to regulate my system and stop the pain and nausea. He basically said the issue was anxiety, stress, and worry.

What?

I was shocked. My mind spiraled with questions: *Seriously? Do they think this is all in my head? Wasn't Mayo Clinic like a medical Mecca? Didn't people who had exhausted all other avenues find their answers here?*

I was pissed. I was totally discouraged. And then I was overcome with shame. I felt like they were telling me that my body wasn't the problem, *I* was the problem.

Then more questions flooded my mind: *God, why did you send me to Mayo? Why did I go through all this, spend all this money, and find out that there was nothing physically wrong with me? Why did you lead me to do this, only for it to be a bust?*

I held out hope that maybe the prescribed medication for anxiety would help, and then I was hit with another question. What was I going to tell my prayer warriors? I told them about my illness and proclaimed my faith and asked for prayers. They had prayed for me and encouraged me. On our last day of our appointments we were overwhelmed with texts and emails from people wanting to know what we learned from the doctors. I wanted to crawl into a hole, just like I did with other difficult situations and challenges in my past. I wanted to remain silent—ignore it all—to stuff it all and hope that everyone would forget.

I asked God why I was led to send out an all-points bulletin to the masses about my health before going to Mayo. I wondered why I professed my faith so openly and asked for prayers. Seriously, Lord? I was utterly humiliated and embarrassed, and my old friend that I knew too well, *shame*, set in even more.

I had no idea how I was going to respond. At dinner that night,

I told David I wanted to ignore everyone who'd reached out, but I knew I couldn't avoid the inevitable. After dinner, we went back to the hotel to craft my message.

I'm from a generation where you don't talk about mental or emotional issues, so you certainly don't send an email to more than 100 people explaining that anxiety/stress was the diagnosis. If a tumor or a disease were the culprit, then I'd have no problem letting everyone know and asking for more prayers. But to say that my mental health had been causing this, geez, I felt—once again—like I was broken.

I was certain that when people discovered my brokenness they'd run the other way. They'd avoid me, ignore me, and talk about me behind my back. All those same emotions I felt when John was killed and when I later divorced after my second marriage were coming back in a slightly different light.

This time, however, rather than ignoring or hiding I made a different choice. After lots of wrestling and choosing the right words, I hit send.

The word was out.

The support was humbling. I received emails back from people saying that they were glad nothing was physically wrong and that their prayers would continue. But, once I returned home, it felt different to me. I sensed that people didn't know what to say when they saw me. Sound familiar?

I remember being in the grocery store and seeing a woman who knew the outcome of this trip—one of my prayer warriors. We briefly locked eyes and then she immediately turned the other direction. That look on her face said everything—that I was broken and she was uncomfortable. Maybe it was just in my imagination, but I was thrown back into emotions from decades before.

Why is this happening again, God? Don't you see your sheep is in distress? Please, God, help me see this entire situation from your perspective.

Even though I didn't like that the doctors diagnosed me with anxiety and stress, I started doing things like yoga, meditation, and exercise per their recommendations. But I still felt horrible. When I looked in a mirror, I saw the skeleton of a person—I was skin and bone.

My illness didn't magically go away. Worse than that, the medication prescribed by the psychiatrist had so many uncomfortable side effects—in addition to the nausea and sleeplessness—that I discontinued it.

I was at the end of my rope.

A few weeks after my return from Mayo in early April 2017, I got a phone call from the gynecologist I saw for unrelated hormonal issues during my round of consults. Come to find out, since I made that appointment, the gynecologist was now included as part of my Mayo medical team.

She told me she reviewed a CT scan that had been sent to them after I'd returned home. The radiologist at Mayo told her that he noticed something odd perforating my uterus. She asked me if I had any idea what that might be. To my embarrassment I realized I'd forgotten to include some information in my health history. It was a complete oversight on my part.

In 2009, I was implanted with a permanent birth control device called Essure. I was tired of taking birth control pills, and my local gynecologist recommended a permanent solution. These were tiny coils inserted into the fallopian tubes. Their purpose was to cause inflammation and scar tissue to develop causing the tubes to close. It was supposed to be a 10-minute office procedure without any downtime, and it seemed like a reasonable thing to do. I set up an appointment without even doing any research for myself.

The procedure failed. Due to some complications, it was only successfully inserted into one fallopian tube—so much for permanent birth control. It requires both fallopian tubes to be implanted in order for it to be effective. I laughed it off. Just another story to add to my weird health challenges.

I was informed that the only way to remove the coil that was successfully implanted was through surgery. At the time, it didn't make sense to pay for an expensive surgery with a lengthy recovery time for some tiny innocent coil, so I declined. I decided to just live with the coil—that was useless anyway—inside of me.

After explaining this to the Mayo gynecologist, she recommended that I talk to my gynecologist in Fayetteville, Arkansas, about Mayo's observations. I reached out to my local doctor, and she said she'd review the scans and let me know her thoughts.

A few days later, my local doctor called and said that it was difficult to see if the uterus was perforated or not. She said that if I was concerned, then she could remove the coil through surgery. It was a standard procedure where she'd remove the fallopian tube and cut/pull the coil from the uterus. I also circled back with the gastroenterologist at Mayo and asked if he thought it had anything to do with my current health situation. He told me that it was probably unrelated.

At that time, I was still so sick and Tyler's graduation was only a few weeks away. So I decided against having the surgery.

My stomach symptoms didn't get better; in fact they started getting worse and getting totally bizarre. My body went haywire. I had random rashes, a constant metallic taste in my mouth, nonstop tingling in my hands and feet, and more. Since I felt like everyone already thought I'd lost my mind, I didn't tell anyone—except for David—about these new symptoms, and I sure as heck wouldn't go to a doctor. Plus, Tyler was graduating in May, and I didn't want anything to take attention from him, so I just kept it all to myself. Just more emotions and information to stuff.

However, deep down, I knew there really was something wrong with me. I believed these symptoms were being caused by *something*. This nausea and sucker punch pain in my gut was not in my head. I knew it in all my being. I was at a loss for what to do next. Even if I was willing to see a doctor, I didn't know which one to turn to. I'd already gone to the best of the best. I felt like

I had already exhausted all medical options. I was out of ideas.

As I wrestled, suffered, cried, and stuffed, I knew there was one friend who knew exactly what was going on. Someone who precisely knew what was making me sick and what would make me healthy. While I was in that lowest of places was when it clicked. God knows everything; he knows what is making me sick. He is my shepherd, and I am his sheep. I'm going to trust him and follow his lead.

I still had one gnawing question in the back of my mind. *God, why did you send me all the way to Mayo?* Despite the question, I continued to reassure myself—he knows, he can heal me—and I kept taking my questions and concerns to him in prayer. Every time some new bizarre symptom would happen, I'd just keep praying.

"God, you know what this is. I trust you. Lead me, I'm your sheep," I'd cry out.

One morning in May 2017, I was having my quiet time, and out of nowhere an acquaintance came to mind. I felt the Lord encouraging me to reach out to her. I knew she had her own health battles and had even gone to Mayo recently. I talked with her before I went to Mayo to learn more about her experience, but I hadn't seen or talked with her since. I wasn't even sure how she was doing.

With lots of graduation preparation and activities, I forgot about that little nudge for a couple of months. Then her name came to mind during my quiet time again in July. I kept putting a note to call her on my to-do list, but I never got around to it.

As only God can orchestrate, I ran into her at the grocery store—and she didn't run the other way. I figured, since I didn't know *why* God kept putting her on my heart, I could at least ask her how she was doing. She told me she was getting so much better and briefly explained what happened after returning from Mayo. We didn't talk long, but she told me that most of her issues were from some implants in her body. Her final comment stopped me in my tracks.

"Theresa, if you have anything foreign in your body, get it out," she said.

What? I do have something foreign in my body. That coil!

As soon as I got to my car I Googled "Essure side effects." I saw words like "complications," "lawsuits," "death," "no longer sold in Canada, Germany, France, Sweden." I even saw that Erin Brockovich, who you may recall was a legal clerk in the 1990s who made a significant impact on a case against PG&E for water contamination that led to widespread unexplained illness, was getting in on the fight against these things.

What the heck? Is this for real?

I felt a nudge, that familiar voice saying, "Theresa, do you see now why I sent you to Mayo?" I realized that God probably sent me to Mayo so that someone would notice the thing that had been in my body for almost 10 years. The thing I'd forgotten about that was potentially perforating my uterus.

As I scrolled my phone and clicked on links, I saw so many symptoms, side effects, and issues similar to mine.

Oh, my gosh. God, you are my shepherd. Is this the thing I've been looking for? Is this the thing that has been making me sick?

I still scratch my head over why I hadn't heard about this from my local doctors and the doctors at Mayo, but since my chief complaint was all about my stomach, the doctors I consulted with were not necessarily thinking about any gynecological issues, and the gynecologists weren't thinking about stomach related issues, either.

I pondered and prayed about this new information and didn't tell anyone for quite a while. I'd slipped back into my stuffing habits after the Mayo trip in March, and I didn't even want to share with David at this point since it seemed a bit far-fetched. Who would believe that something that had been in my body for nearly a decade could be the culprit?

However, I continued my research. I knew to be careful and selective in the websites I visited. Experience had taught me that I could be led down some rabbit holes if I wasn't mindful of my information sources. To my surprise, I found medical journals, manufacturer instruction manuals, articles written by reputable doctors from reputable hospitals, and more referring to Essure and its potential issues.

I shared this information with my sister, who's a registered nurse. I asked her to review what I'd found to make sure I wasn't being misled—or in my hopes for answers seeing connections that didn't exist. After our research we both concluded that this was *no* joke. I had a potential ticking time bomb in my body.

The further I researched, the more I realized that this device had been banned from nearly every country in the world *except* the US. In addition, within the previous couple of years, the FDA had placed a black box warning on the device for life-threatening risks and side effects.

I also found a private Facebook group of nearly 35,000 women who had the Essure procedure and were suffering from side effects. I joined the group and began to read thousands of stories of all kinds of medical issues, some of which were very similar to mine.

My latest question: How do I get rid of this thing?

The more I dug, the more I came to understand that the most comprehensive way to remove the coil was to have a complete hysterectomy. You see, the coil has multiple components. It's not only a coil. It also includes fibers that are designed to cause inflammation and scar tissue to form. If these fibers go astray, which can happen if the coil is pulled or cut, then they can cause scar tissue and inflammation wherever they ended up. If that was the case, I just wanted it and everything around it to be removed from my body.

Good grief. I need my shepherd even more.

I continued to pray and trust and believe that my shepherd was directing me. Every step of the way, I looked toward him. Every doctor I met with, I looked to God. Every piece of new information I found, I looked to God. Although options were presented to me to remove only the fallopian tube where the coil was inserted, I felt to my core that I needed a complete hysterectomy. It was just an instinct. Looking back, I believe that was my shepherd nudging me on how to best handle this situation. Once again, God was at work.

On October 5, 2017—my twenty-sixth wedding anniversary—David and I arrived very early in the morning for my scheduled laparoscopic hysterectomy. I felt at peace (Philippians 4:6-7). I knew God was with me and that he called me to be strong and courageous (Joshua 1:9). Regardless of whether this thing was causing me all the issues, I'd be rid of it.

The surgery went well, and that evening the surgeon stopped by my hospital room and showed me pictures where the coil not only had perforated my uterus but had migrated and was attached to the outside of my uterus in my abdominal cavity. None of the doctors had speculated about that before the surgery. We were all blown away. A complete hysterectomy was the right thing to do.

I went home the next day, and I finally felt like I was on the road to recovery. The first thing I noticed was that those bizarre symptoms I experienced after returning from Mayo, like rashes and that disgusting metallic taste, were gone in a matter of days, and that tingle in my extremities that was driving me nuts was gone as well.

I had to remind myself that it took nearly ten years for my body to get to its current state, so my complete recovery might take longer. I'd need to be patient. Over time, the stomach issues and nausea disappeared, and the pain subsided and eventually was gone.

I often wonder if the stomach issues and nausea were due to the inflammation caused by the coil in my abdominal cavity. Only God knows that for sure. But I do know this: my shepherd guided me through this crazy journey. Had I not gotten to the point of desperation and realized I needed to trust only my shepherd, I might still have this thing in my body wreaking more havoc.

If I wasn't in a place of surrender and desperately seeking his direction, I don't think I would've felt his nudge to talk to my friend in the grocery store or to make a random appointment to see a gynecologist at Mayo. No, I don't think these are just coincidences—more like God-incidences.

I'll never know for sure. But to me, it was my shepherd who heard my cries and led me to my healing (Psalm 116:1).

My part was, and is, to play the role of the sheep and trust God, because he is my shepherd. He knows best, and I'm following his lead. Even when my circumstances don't immediately change, I've learned to wait patiently on him. His plan will unfold according to his timing and his ways.

I can't put into words any better how I feel than the words in Psalm 23:

> The Lord is my shepherd; I shall not want.
> He makes me lie down in green pastures.
> He leads me beside still waters.
> He restores my soul.
> He leads me in paths of righteousness
> for his name's sake.
>
> Even though I walk through the valley of the shadow of death,
>   I will fear no evil,
> for you are with me;
>   your rod and your staff,
>   they comfort me.
>
> You prepare a table before me
>   in the presence of my enemies;
> you anoint my head with oil;
>   my cup overflows.
> Surely goodness and mercy shall follow me
>   all the days of my life,
> and I shall dwell in the house of the Lord
>   forever. (Psalm 23)

Insights and Scriptures to Trust God
EVERYDAY APPLICATIONS

What I learned:

1. God is my shepherd and cares about me intimately and deeply. Even though he is the creator of *all* things, he is *my* shepherd and invites me to be his sheep.

2. We all struggle with one or more of the qualities of a sheep: stubborn, selfish, strong-willed, afraid, discontent, skeptical. That's okay. Embrace my "sheepness."

3. Follow my shepherd. God is in control, and he knows what is best for me. Stop trying to be the leader, and let him lead.

4. Surrender to my shepherd. Surrender to his plans, realize that his ways and his timing for my life are perfect.

5. Trust that God has plans for me and that he will direct and lead me on the right path. Be confident that he will lead.

6. Seek God's outlook. We all have a limited point of view on our circumstances, but God sees it all. Pray that he will show me his perspective on my situation.

7. Connect with my shepherd constantly, since I am in God's constant care. Create a discipline to read his Word, pray, memorize Scripture, and worship him. Know God more intimately—he already knows everything about me.

8. When challenging circumstances come my way, just do what I know to do: keep on trusting, stay close to the Lord, be vulnerable with him, seek his wisdom in his Word, and never cease praying.

Scriptures that led to these insights:

- For this is what the Sovereign Lord says: I myself will search for my sheep and look after them. As a shepherd looks after his scattered flock when he is with them, so will I look after my sheep. (Ezekiel 34:11-12)

- We all, like sheep, have gone astray, each of us has turned to our own way. (Isaiah 53:6)

- Trust in the Lord with all your heart, lean not on your own understanding; in all your ways submit to him, and he will make your paths straight. (Proverbs 3:5-6)

- Do not be anxious about anything, but in every situation, by prayer and petition, with thanksgiving, present your requests to God. And the peace of God, which transcends all understanding, will guard your hearts and minds in Christ Jesus. (Philippians 4:6-7)

- Have I not commanded you? Be strong and courageous. Do not be afraid; do not be discouraged, for the Lord your God will be with you wherever you go. (Joshua 1:9)

- I love the Lord, for he heard my voice; he heard my cry for mercy. (Psalm 116:1)

Chapter 8

INSIGHT 5: FORGIVE—
EVEN WHEN IT'S HARD

When I began this journey in 2016, I didn't realize that the way I handled life's challenges was hurting me physically, emotionally, and spiritually. Stuffing my pain was like sticking my head in the sand and ignoring that there were problems. Thinking that burying any loss, hurt, and resulting emotions would make them magically go away over time was naïve. I was creating much nastier wounds by not addressing them in the first place, but I didn't see it that way at the time.

A few years ago, I read a children's book called *What Do You Do With A Problem?*[1] Bethany, my son Dylan's fiancée (now his wife), posted it on social media as a book recommendation for parents. At the time, she was a kindergarten teacher. Out of curiosity, I picked

---

[1] Kobi Yamada (author), Mae Besom (illustrator), *What Do You Do With a Problem?* (Seattle, WA: Compendium Publishing, 2016).

it up and read it while I was in a bookstore. I saw myself in those pages—how the little boy tried to hide from the problem, and how he wanted to avoid it and wished it would disappear, looked all too familiar.

As a result of these patterns to avoid and ignore any issues, I collected loads of unresolved hurts that I'd stored inside me. Along with the impact of any original hurts, I started holding on to other emotions like anger, bitterness, and resentment. Those feelings overwhelmed and scared me.

Whenever I had the courage to search inside myself and try to address them, I couldn't deal with what I felt. So I'd shut that door again, stuff my emotions even further, and go on with life. I was hoping they'd eventually go away on their own.

Suppressed sadness, grief, anger, bitterness, and resentment can be incredibly harmful. They can eat at you if you don't deal with them.

I felt stuck—stuck with unresolved wounds and emotions and now experiencing health issues, to boot. However, I was uncertain how to address these.

In Chapter 3, I mentioned that David's mentor Tim suggested that burying my pain might be causing my health issues. Even though Tim's response didn't sit well, I knew his intentions were good. Thankfully, instead of ignoring and avoiding his comment, I chose to step into it. I began praying to see my situation from God's perspective. God already knew everything about me and my entire life history, so I felt confident that he'd direct me in this new exploration.

At the time, I was in a group Bible study, and as God so perfectly orchestrated, we were reading the Gospel of John. In John 14, I read something that gave me pause. It said, "If you love me, you will obey my commands." In several verses, I read that we show our love for God by obeying his Word (John 14:15, 21, 23).

I was uncertain why I felt so unsettled over these verses. I love

God. I knew I wasn't perfect. No one is. So I prayed for God to show me where I was being disobedient. In the back of my mind, though, I wondered if this had to do with buried wounds and my current health situation.

One day, in a deep time of prayer and reflection, one word came to mind: forgiveness. Then reality hit me broadside. Since I chose to stuff many hurts and hold on to unresolved pain, I'd never forgiven the offense or the offender—I just chose to bury it instead.

Whoa! Now, that got my attention.

God calls us to forgive, just like he forgives us of all of our sins. Scriptures tell us that. A particular verse that comes to mind says to bear with each other and forgive one another as the Lord has forgiven us (Colossians 3:13).

So I asked myself, "Do I forgive as God forgives me? Or do I avoid dealing with an offense, letting it linger in my heart and as a result hold on to unforgiveness?"

As I sat there, I was overwhelmed with a gut-wrenching reality. By stuffing all the hurts and leaving them unresolved, I hadn't followed God's instruction on forgiveness in his Word. That was where I was being disobedient, and I could no longer ignore that.

Since then, I've learned that we have to approach forgiveness from a different direction to move forward. And that's between ourselves and the Lord.

I had a multidecade load of hurts and unforgiveness that I collected simply because I was afraid to address issues when they occurred, and I was uncertain what to do with it all now that I was ready to face it. My boatload of unforgiveness had taken on a life of its own, and it was buried deep inside of me. Fortunately, I was determined to get it out.

That's where my journey of forgiveness began. I wish I could say that it was a one-and-done deal. I had to go back to many hurts, to feel them again and consciously forgive others *and* myself—sometimes multiple times. I remember one morning sitting in my quiet time chair and praying through old offenses as they were flooding my mind.

I found myself forgiving anyone and everyone who popped into my head. Obviously, it started with the terrorists who killed John, but it didn't end there. My mind was flooded with experiences and people where I'd held on to unresolved hurts for far too long. That included people from many seasons of my life.

After that, I thought all my old wounds were healed—unforgiveness was no more. Then something would happen to trigger a memory of an old hurt, and I was right back feeling unresolved pain and anger all over again. It was the same pattern I experienced when I recognized my true enemy—I take a step forward, and Satan whispers lies and doubts.

This cycle went on for months.

I was frustrated. I felt like I'd forgiven out of obedience to God, but I was still tormented with all the emotions that I'd left unresolved for so long. I felt captive to my past hurts. I cried out to God in prayer to help me know what to do with the emotions that I still struggled with.

As an answer to that prayer, Tim asked David if I'd be willing to meet with him face-to-face. I was apprehensive from the sting of his comment to David a few months earlier, but I agreed. Tim asked me to bring my Bible and when we met, he asked me to read aloud, Matthew 18:23-35, the story of the unforgiving debtor.

The story starts with a king who decided to collect from everyone who owed him money. One of the men, who had a substantial debt, couldn't pay it back, so the king planned to throw him in prison until his debt was paid. The man pleaded with the king, who showed great compassion and forgave the man's debt.

Afterward, the forgiven man went to all those who owed him money and asked them to pay back their debts. Unlike the king, the man showed no mercy and threw a man who owed him money in prison. People in town heard about this and told the king, who was furious. In response, the king threw the man he had originally forgiven into prison.

The story ends with a lesson that God will treat anyone who doesn't forgive others the same way. They, too, will be thrown into a prison, of sorts.

I wanted to understand what I could learn from this story. Even though I didn't like the thought of being compared to the unforgiving man, I knew I had to be honest with myself.

Regardless of all my pain, I understood that my responsibility was to forgive as an act of obedience to God. However, I thought I'd already forgiven months before, but this story explained that I needed to take it even further.

Our call to forgive can't depend on someone else admitting their wrong or making things right. While we often want something in return for the hurt we experience from others *before* we forgive—remorse, apology, some level of justice, a change in their behavior, or accountability—God's instruction is different.

God forgives us despite all our debts, and he expects us to extend the same forgiveness to others despite any debt they may owe to us. We're called to forgive *and* to release those who hurt us from their debt.

Tim Keller, the late pastor and best-selling author, gave a profound perspective on this in his book *The Reason for God.*[2] He said, "Forgiveness means refusing to make them pay for what they did." He continued, "You are absorbing the debt, taking the cost of it completely on yourself instead of taking it out on the other person. It hurts terribly. Many people would say it feels like a kind of death. Yes, but it is a death that leads to resurrection instead of the lifelong living death of bitterness and cynicism" (p. 188-189).

Letting go of a debt for some harm against you may be incredibly difficult and even painful. I get that. But by forgiving that

---

[2] Timothy Keller, *The Reason for God: Belief in an Age of Skepticism* (New York: Penguin Books, 2008).

debt we're ending a potential cycle of trying to get payment through revenge, retaliation, or hanging on to unforgiveness and bitterness.

As I continued to reflect on the unforgiving debtor, I thought about how God calls us to bless those who persecute us (Romans 12:14 AMP). This suggests that even after we forgive and release those who wronged us, we must also bless them.

I had to wrestle with this idea. I may forgive and release, but bless as well? I wasn't sure I had that in me, but God assures me that his grace is sufficient to give me his strength in my weakness (2 Corinthians 12:9). He can put those hurts behind me and in their proper perspective.

If Jesus is our model for living a godly life, think about all the hurtful and harmful actions that happened to him before he forgave us while hanging on the cross (Luke 23:34). Can you imagine what a pickle we'd all be in if he said he didn't forgive humanity until everyone who insulted him, hit him, scourged him, humiliated him, and crucified him first had to apologize and show remorse?

God calls us to forgive those who hurt us, release them from anything we think they owe us, *and* bless them. That is obedience to God. That shows our love for him.

That's what he calls us to do—all of it.

And what about the prison reference in the story? I wanted to understand what that implied and how it applied to me. While I was pondering this, I saw a Tweet on Twitter that hit home. Craig Groeschel, the pastor of Life Church based in Oklahoma City, tweeted, "Unforgiveness is choosing to stay trapped in a prison of bitterness, serving time for someone else's crime."[3]

Yikes.

I'd buried wounds in reaction to my inability to handle pain and conflict. By not addressing each situation as it occurred, I allowed unforgiveness and bitterness to set in. Those emotions were hurting me—not the person who caused the hurt in the first place.

---

[3] Twitter, (@craiggroeschel, posted October 31, 2021.

Yes, I was the prisoner. I thought that the bitterness and resentment I felt were justified. I thought hanging on to all those hurts would somehow make those who hurt me feel bad for what they did and prompt them to make amends, but it did the opposite.

Hanging on to my emotions caused me to be the one who was imprisoned, captive, and suffering. As a result, I was unable to move forward with my life and experience the freedom that forgiveness provides.

I knew that I no longer wanted to be in an emotional prison for hurt caused by someone else. I didn't want to feel powerless or wait for someone else to make things right.

So I was back in my prayer chair again. This time, I wrote down my long-neglected hurts and wounds on separate pieces of paper.

When I finished, I got up, found a bucket, went outside in the rain, and burned each one.

With each scrap, I offered up a prayer of forgiveness. "Lord Jesus, I forgive, I release them from their debt, and I pray for a blessing on them."

Then I went back to the throne of God Almighty and asked him to release me, to forgive me for my unforgiving heart.

I still occasionally experience triggers that bring an old wound to mind, and unforgiveness rears its ugly head again. The enemy is trying to lure me back to that emotional prison.

When that happens, I follow the advice given by Sean Vollendorf, a director at StuMo (short for Student Mobilization) college ministry, who spoke at our church a few years ago. He shared a personal challenge he experienced with unforgiveness and suggested that if something triggers the memory of an offense after you've already forgiven, then to do something he called "rinse and repeat"—keep on forgiving as many times as your heart continues to bring it up.

God says we aren't called to forgive only once or twice but "seventy times seven" (Matthew 18:21-22 NLT), and that doesn't mean 490 times, for those of you who are quick with your mental math skills. It means to forgive and keep on forgiving without limits. Keep taking it to the Lord and laying it at his feet. It's helpful whenever old wounds come up—to dispel any harmful emotions that unexpectedly arise.

Yes, forgiveness is a decision. When it felt impossible, I had to choose to come to a place where I looked forward instead of dwelling on the past and holding on to unforgiveness.

Even when my heart was on board to forgive, my head still needed some convincing.

Here are some of the issues I wrestled with before I could move forward—in case you find yourself in a similar place:

First, forgiveness is for something done in the past.

Let's face it: the past can't be changed. So let that be part of your reasoning for forgiving the offense. Holding onto it only hurts *you*. I love the Bible verse that says to forget the former things and don't dwell on the past (Isaiah 43:18). I believe God knows that we easily get stuck by dwelling on something that can't be changed.

Second, forgiving someone doesn't mean that you condone or approve their actions. Nor does it suggest that their behavior is acceptable.

Many people refuse to forgive because they think it implies that they were never wronged. The opposite is true. If there was no offense, then forgiveness would be unnecessary. Forgiving requires acknowledging the offense and pardoning the offender.

Third, you shouldn't confuse forgiveness with trust and reconciliation.

We're called to forgive, but we aren't called to be a doormat. These are separate matters. Obviously, when someone hurts you, your trust in that person may be compromised, and when that happens, you may find it hard to forgive. You may even feel like you have to trust them *first*, but you don't. Even when your trust has been broken, you can forgive the offense—and choose to never trust them again.

Trust is earned and involves two people. It requires work from both parties to come to a place of restoration and make things right. If you want reconciliation, then you must first have open communication.

There are Scriptures that support communicating the offense to promote a healthy relationship. Matthew 18:15 says, "If your brother sins against you, go and tell him his fault, between you and him alone. If he listens to you, you have gained your brother." God's Word is clear. If someone hurts you, *go and talk to them*. Forget about waiting for the other person to take the first step.

Keep in mind though, *how* you communicate is also very important to the outcome of the conversation and your relationship. Scripture says that if someone sins against us then we're to restore them *gently* (Galatians 6:1). We're called to speak truth, even when it's hard truth, in a spirit of love.

Truth is sometimes hard to say, and can certainly be hard to hear. But even when truth is hard it doesn't have to be delivered in a spirit of meanness. The best chance for a positive outcome is to confront someone in a loving manner, in the hope for resolution, not harm.

Regardless of whether trust and reconciliation are desired or restored, the important thing to understand is that your obedience to forgive isn't tied to anyone else acknowledging the hurt or working to restore the relationship.

Forgiveness requires one person—*you*. It is a decision between you and God, and it will open the door to your healing.

I want to be clear that I'm not minimizing or excusing any pain or hurt you've experienced. Nor am I justifying any type of abuse, harm, or mistreatment done against you. Regardless of what wounds you've experienced in your life, the emotions you carry are real and can often be paralyzing and frightening. And this is why it's important not to put our own healing in someone else's hands.

Maybe you've been hurt in unimaginable ways, and forgiveness is a struggle. Maybe everything that I've written in this chapter feels nearly impossible. I encourage you to find someone you trust—a therapist, counselor, or trusted friend—to process these hurts with you. Don't wrestle with this alone.

Ask God to give you his perspective on your situation. Ask him to soften your heart. This is a process, and it may take time, but don't give up on yourself. Keep moving toward a place where you can *choose* to forgive. It's where *your* healing can begin and you can experience freedom from emotions that are holding on to you.

We're all imperfect humans. We're all sinners and fall short of the glory of God—every single day (Romans 3:23-24). Regardless of who hurts us, why they did it, or the pain that they have caused us, we're called to forgive because God forgives each of us. Our forgiveness is an act of worship and obedience to God.

Think of it this way: we forgive others not because they deserve it but because God knows *you* deserve it and he wants *you* to be free.

Insights and Scriptures to Forgive—Even When It's Hard
EVERYDAY APPLICATIONS

What I learned about struggling with unforgiveness

1. Show my love to God by being obedient to his commands.

2. God calls me to forgive, release, *and* bless those who hurt me from anything I think they owe me. That is obedience to God and shows my love for him.

3. Approach forgiveness from a different direction to move forward. Forgiveness is between me and the Lord.

4. God forgives me despite my debts, and he expects me to extend the same forgiveness to others.

5. Unforgiveness puts me in an emotional prison. Hanging on to painful emotions only hurts me—not those who've hurt me— and can prevent me from experiencing the freedom of forgiveness.

6. Sometimes triggers can bring back old wounds. If that happens, "rinse and repeat." Keep taking it to the feet of Jesus as many times as my heart requires.

7. Forgiveness is for something done in the past. Since I can't change the past, let that be part of my reasoning for forgiving the offense.

8. Forgiveness doesn't mean I condone the action. My act of forgiveness doesn't mean I approve of the hurt.

9. I shouldn't confuse forgiveness with trust and reconciliation. They are separate matters. When I'm hurt, trust is compromised. Trust is earned. Trust takes work from both parties.

10. Forgive others, not because they deserve it but because God knows I deserve it, and he wants me to be free.

Scriptures that led me to these insights

- For the Spirit God gave us does not make us timid, but gives us power, love and self-discipline. (2 Timothy 1:7)

- "If you love me, keep my commands." (John 14:15)

- "Whoever has my commands and keeps them is the one who loves me. The one who loves me will be loved by my Father, and I too will love them and show myself to them." (John 14:21)

- Jesus replied, "Anyone who loves me will obey my teaching. My Father will love them, and we will come to them and make our home with them." (John 14:23 John 14:23)

- Bear with each other and forgive one another if any of you has a grievance against someone. Forgive as the Lord forgave you. (Colossians 3:13)

- "Therefore, the kingdom of heaven is like a king who wanted to settle accounts with his servants. As he began the settlement, a man who owed him ten thousand bags of gold was brought to him. Since he was not able to pay, the master ordered that he and his wife and his children and all that he had be sold to repay the debt. At this, the servant fell on his knees before him. 'Be patient with me,' he begged, 'and I will pay back everything.' The servant's master took pity on him, canceled the debt, and let him go. But when that servant went out, he found one of his fellow servants who owed him a hundred silver coins. He grabbed him and began to choke him. 'Pay back what you owe me!' he demanded. His fellow servant fell to his knees and begged him, 'Be patient with me, and I will pay it back.' But he refused. Instead, he went off and had the man thrown into prison until he could pay the debt. When the other servants saw what had happened, they were outraged and went and told their master everything that had happened. Then the master called the servant in. 'You wicked servant,' he said, 'I canceled all that debt of yours because you begged me to. Shouldn't you have had mercy on your fellow servant just as I had on you?' In anger, his master handed him over to the jailers to be tortured until he should pay back all he owed. This is how my heavenly Father will treat each of you unless you forgive your brother or sister from your heart." (Matthew 18:23-35)

- Bless those who persecute you [who cause you harm or hardship]; bless and do not curse [them]. (Romans 12:14 AMP)

- But he said to me, "My grace is sufficient for you, for my power is made perfect in weakness." Therefore I will boast all the more gladly about my weaknesses, so that Christ's power may rest on me. (2 Corinthians 12:9)

- Jesus said, "Father, forgive them, for they do not know what they are doing." (Luke 23:34)

- Then Peter came to him and asked, "Lord, how often should I forgive someone who sins against me? Seven times?" "No, not seven times," Jesus replied, "but seventy times seven!" (Matthew 18:21-22 NLT)

- "Forget the former things; do not dwell on the past." (Isaiah 43:18)

- "If your brother or sister sins, go and point out their fault, just between the two of you. If they listen to you, you have won them over." (Matthew 18:15)

- Brothers and sisters, if someone is caught in a sin, you who live by the Spirit should restore that person gently. (Galatians 6:1)

- "Therefore, if you are offering your gift at the altar and there remember that your brother or sister has something against you, leave your gift there in front of the altar. First go and be reconciled to them; then come and offer your gift." (Matthew 5:23-24)

- Therefore, confess your sins to one another [your false steps, your offenses], and pray for one another, that you may be healed *and* restored. (James 5:16 AMP)
- For all have sinned and fall short of the glory of God, and all are justified freely by his grace through the redemption that came by Christ Jesus. (Romans 3:23-24)

Chapter 9

INSIGHT 6: GET BETTER, NOT BITTER

Forgiveness was a necessary step for my own healing. Through my obedience to God to forgive, the painful emotions I stuffed came to the surface. I soon realized that uncovering the emotions and processing them were two separate issues, and looking back, I'd only accomplished the first.

I was still wrestling with anger, bitterness, and resentment. Those emotions distorted my feelings toward people who'd hurt me. They even intensified my reactions to new circumstances, and no amount of the "rinse and repeat" practice I mentioned in the previous chapter worked.

I wanted to become a healthier version of myself.

Stuffing unwanted feelings and ignoring difficult situations was harmful, but simply forgiving an offense without addressing its impact and processing the emotions is incomplete. It's a way of avoiding critical work God wants us to do.

We know in this life there will be problems (John 16:33). I wanted to figure out how to deal with life's problems so that I could put my past behind me and more effectively deal with future challenges.

There was more to this journey, so I pushed forward. I was determined to move on from the hurts I'd buried and turn toward what God planned for me *now*.

Journaling—one of my quiet time practices—allowed me to more clearly see what was in my heart and head and start making sense of some of the emotions I felt, but it only helped to a certain extent.

Since I'd never addressed many of my painful experiences, I wasn't even sure my emotions made sense. I didn't know if they were justified or even accurate. And, when I identified specific emotions, I didn't know what to do with them.

That's when I realized that I had to find someone who could walk through my mess with me and help me come to terms with it.

I applaud younger generations who explore their mental health and embrace the expertise of counselors and therapists. It seems like people in my generation kept our feelings to ourselves to outwardly appear strong.

I was hesitant to look for help, but I was desperate to put my pain behind me. It was important for me to find a licensed counselor with a Christian background who would lean on both his expertise and his faith when providing wisdom and counsel.

When I found the right fit and we began meeting, I shared my personal story, and I explained that I was still having a hard time letting the past go. I told him I wanted to be able to look at these experiences with a heart of acceptance and move forward in my life—to come to a place of emotional and relational health.

We started by discussing the emotions that I felt. I explained that even after I faced the hurts I'd stuffed, I continued feeling angry and bitter. I felt powerless against the memories and helpless against the emotions. I was in a vicious cycle, and I felt captive. I was just stuck.

Anger is only one of many human emotions. It is a signal that there is a problem. It's our mind's way of saying, "Hey, something isn't right here." I chose to ignore my anger and stuff it over the years. I learned that when anger is left unresolved, bitterness and resentment eventually come along to keep it company.

It's not a healthy threesome, that's for sure.

These emotions had taken up camp inside of me, which made it hard to move past the original problem that caused the hurt and the anger in the first place.

I wanted a biblical understanding of anger, bitterness, and resentment, so I dug deep into God's Word, and there was plenty about them. Bible reference sites (Biblegateway.com and Biblehub. com, for example) make it easy to find Scriptures addressing those emotions.

Several Bible verses advise us to be slow to anger (Proverbs 14:29 ESV, Proverbs 19:11 ESV). I also read that anger, left unchecked, doesn't produce the righteous living that God desires in us (James 1:19-20). The Apostle Paul instructs the Ephesians to deal with anger immediately and not let Satan get a foothold on it (Ephesians 4:26-27), and Psalms tells us that anger without self-control can lead to harm (Psalm 37:8 NKJV).

I don't believe these Scriptures say that anger is bad or wrong. Even Jesus felt righteous anger when the people were being taken advantage of in the temple. But what these Scriptures address is what we *do* with our anger.

Burying and ignoring anger are *not* included as healthy coping strategies.

These instructions were helpful, and they might work well for future issues, but it was also clear that how I handled my anger—by stuffing it—was part of the problem. It wasn't aligned with what Scripture teaches us to do when we're faced with difficult situations.

Next, I started exploring biblical direction on bitterness and resentment.

As I searched the Bible once again, Scriptures taught me to be careful that no root of bitterness should spring up or cause trouble (Hebrews 12:15 NLT).

If you know anything about plants, you know they can't live without roots. Such is the case for bitterness. It can't exist if you don't let it set root in your heart. But, since I'd allowed it to set root, then the instruction was very straightforward—dig it up (Ephesians 4:31 NLT).

After my biblical deep dive, I realized that these emotions were causing me more harm than good. The hard truth was that holding onto anger about situations in the past resulted in bitterness, leading me to an unforgiving heart and a negative and critical attitude—especially toward those who'd caused me pain.

My heart was wounded, and that hurt was real. But choosing to stuff it and not deal with it promptly meant my heart had hardened. That was more than likely why no amount of "rinse and repeat" of forgiveness was going to work.

There isn't anything good about feeling bitter and resentful. It just perpetuates the hurt. Carrie Fisher, the late author, actress, and screenwriter, wrote in her autobiography, *Wishful Drinking*,[1] "Resentment is like drinking poison and waiting for the other person to die."[2] Holding on to bitterness only causes you additional pain and doesn't affect the person who hurt you, in the first place.

I was at a crossroads. Would I be obedient to God's Word and rid myself of all my anger, bitterness, and resentment? Or would I hang onto it and let it poison me further?

---

[1] Carrie Fisher, *Wishful Drinking* (New York: Simon & Schuster, 2008).
[2] I don't know where the quote originated. I've seen it attributed to sources as varied as twelve step programs, Malachy McCourt, and Saint Augustine. Fisher uses it in her book on p. 153.

Obviously, I wanted to get rid of it, but it wasn't as easy as snapping my fingers. I tried that, but then a memory would remind me of an offense, and I'd feel all those emotions again—as if all the time I'd already spent in prayer and forgiveness had never happened.

Why in the world was I still battling?

I was still stumped, so my counselor and I continued examining it. I shared that I felt powerless. I felt like I had no control over my emotions nor was I responsible for them—those who hurt me were responsible.

That's where my counselor set me straight about feelings and emotions. He shared that although others may have caused me hurt, I'm responsible for the emotions I feel now. He referenced the book *Boundaries*[3], where Dr. Henry Cloud and Dr. John Townsend describe that our feelings, emotions, attitudes, thoughts, and behaviors are our property—they define who we are. Therefore, we're responsible for and must own them.

Yes, the wrongs against me caused me great pain, no doubt. No one is saying anything different. But I was confused because I thought something or someone outside of me was responsible for my continued anger and bitterness, and for those emotions to go away, something or someone outside me had to do something to make things right.

It was the same lesson my mom had given me when I first moved to North Carolina, "Theresa, no one can make you happy. *You* have to make yourself happy."

I'd put my healing and happiness in someone else's hands. One was a terrorist who died in that horrific bombing, others were no longer part of my life, and some were still in my life, but I knew I didn't have the courage to address the hurt with them. In each case, I'd given someone else *my* power and put my healing in an impossible predicament.

---

[3] Henry Cloud, John Townsend, *Boundaries: When to Say Yes, How to Say No to Take Control of Your Life* (Grand Rapids: Zondervan, 1992).

I had to accept that my healing isn't dependent on anyone else. I had a choice here. I had the power to let go of the painful emotions I felt. Although I didn't cause the past hurts, I was responsible for my response going forward.

That simple shift of responsibility back to myself returned my power.

I used to feel like my emotions had a mind of their own, but if I'm responsible for my feelings, then I no longer have to be a victim of my stuffed hurts or the emotions that tormented me. Instead, I could be in control.

But that meant I had to face them head-on and resolve them.

I asked my counselor how to let these issues go. How do I finally get rid of the pent-up anger, bitterness, and resentment? And he shared a few helpful thoughts.

First, he suggested that I do some personal work to see if God would give me any new perspective—to pray for God to broaden my limited perspective with his perspective and provide wisdom on things that have troubled me (James 1:5 ESV). This change in perspective, also called reframing, could help me begin to see things differently and move toward resolving and letting go of the hurt.

After spending some time in prayer, I was reminded that God works in all things for the good of those who love him (Romans 8:28). I'm not saying that these hurts were good, by any stretch of the imagination, or that God caused them. Instead, this Bible verse assures us that God is working for our good, even in our most difficult circumstances.

I realized that God used those experiences to shape me to be more like Jesus—to give me greater empathy to comfort those who have endured deep pain and have the heart to help others who struggle with facing their pain and avoiding or burying their hurts (2 Corinthians 1:3-4). These experiences have given me an extra measure of perseverance, strength, and compassion for others.

In addition, this shift in mindset also helped me see that I've learned some important lessons through many of my most trying times. I know learning something positive may seem counterintuitive in a negative situation, but hurtful experiences can teach us things, too—like how we *don't* want to treat others and what type of person we *don't* want to be.

Next, my counselor suggested that I pray for God to show me if my own attitudes or behaviors contributed to any emotions that were still troubling me. Hear me out—he wasn't insinuating that my attitudes or behaviors contributed to the original hurt. Instead, he suggested that I pray for God to reveal if my current emotions and attitudes contributed to the ongoing bitterness I felt.

I love the verse that asks God to search our hearts and let us know if there is anything in us that's offensive (Psalm 139:23-24). This is such a good verse to meditate on. We're often blind to our own weaknesses. We may not see it, but God sure does. We need to own it, and if we determine it's part of the problem, then we need to address it.

Painfully, I was led to the story about the Prodigal son in the Gospel of Luke (Luke 15:11-32). The story is about two brothers. The younger brother asks for his portion of his father's inheritance (while his dad is still alive) and then squanders it all and becomes destitute. He returns home in shame and plans to admit his sin and beg his father to take him in as a servant, but to his surprise, his father welcomes him with open arms and holds a huge celebration in his honor.

Meanwhile, his older brother is seething with jealousy after he hears his father's response. The older brother was doing the right thing but didn't feel like he was given what he thought he deserved for his loyalty. He was consumed with pride, self-righteousness, and anger. He thought he was being unfairly treated, and he was ticked off by his younger brother. Rather than his prodigal brother getting what he deserved, he was shown grace, mercy, and forgiveness. And that didn't sit well with the older brother.

Yikes.

How many times have I read that story and was unaffected by it? But this time, I was struck by the realization that perhaps I was a lot like the older brother. Just like the older brother was angry at his father for how he treated his younger brother, am I somehow upset with God for how he chooses to deal with those who caused me pain? Do I have an attitude of pride and self-righteousness by thinking that my holding onto bitterness and resentment are justified?

Through the years, I've looked at my situation, thinking I played no part in the painful emotions I experienced. But my ongoing pain has less to do with the original offenses and more to do with choosing not to face the unresolved pain and hurts and holding on to unforgiveness and bitterness.

I'd gotten myself into this predicament.

I'd been bitter and wrestling with an unforgiving heart because I wanted to get what I thought I deserved. I wanted to see God avenge me. He says that he will (Romans 12:17-19). But I had to accept that God's discipline happens in his way and in his timing, not mine. If I believe that God is always at work for our good, then I have to *trust* that he's at work in those who caused those wounds, just like he's at work in me.

The beautiful thing is that this mindset shifts the responsibility for getting what I feel like I deserve away from my hands and places it in the right hands—God's.

There is so much freedom in this.

Freedom was what I yearned for then, and what I continue to cultivate now. I no longer have to figure out how to get what I deserve or how to prove my case. That's God's job, and I'm releasing that to him.

I realized that I played a role in my ongoing battle with bitterness. I couldn't overlook the fact that I needed to ask for God's forgiveness for myself—for holding onto these emotions. Even though I thought they were justified, they weren't.

I also realized that I had to confess my self-righteousness and pride. Thinking my resentment and bitterness were justified led me to those attitudes, and they have bled into how I've treated others and mishandled other issues.

Who's to say that's not what God has been waiting for from me all these years to free me from my pain? But I want to be right with God, and to do that, I've got to release my bitterness and anger, lay it at His feet, and let it go.

Josh Shipp, a motivational speaker and best-selling author, talks about our choice to let go. He said, "You either get bitter or you get better. It's that simple. You either take what has been dealt to you and allow it to make you a better person, or you allow it to tear you down. The choice does not belong to fate, it belongs to you."[4]

So it was time for me to have a big slice of humble pie here. Get rid of all that bitterness that caused me and others pain, and take on a heart of humility.

We all have flaws, and I'm included. That's the nature of humanity. So, just as the prodigal son's father showed him grace and mercy when he returned home penniless and repentant, I have to do the same. Now that I clearly see my own faults (or at least see them more often), that's what I want to receive from our heavenly Father as well—his grace and mercy.

I'd come to a pivotal point in my journey. I'd done my best to forgive, release, and bless. I'd done my best to let go of the bitterness I held onto. But there was one more crucial step—acceptance.

Acceptance looks at these situations in a nonjudgmental way. I can't change what has already happened to me. If I want to move forward, then I have to accept those difficult parts of my life and acknowledge and embrace them without judgment.

My older son, Dylan, had a saying in high school that we've all adopted in our family. He often said, "It is what it is," when challenging things would occur. Several years ago, he wrote about that state-

---

[4] I don't know if this quote originated in one of his books or as part of a talk, but it's all over social media. A quick Google search will produce dozens of images.

ment in one of his college entrance essays, explaining that when he faced a difficult situation outside of his control, he learned to just accept it. It allowed him to move forward and not get stuck wrestling over it or wanting circumstances to be different.

As I looked over all the hurts I'd stuffed and avoided in my life, I realized I had a choice. I could continue kicking and screaming about these old wounds and making myself miserable, or I could simply accept these circumstances as part of my story.

I'm choosing to accept the past that I can't change and let go of the bitterness that had a grip on me. I'm choosing to see that even though these were painful experiences, they're part of my story and they've shaped me into the loving, caring, and compassionate person that I am today.

Now I can look forward to what tomorrow brings. I can move on with what lies ahead for my life and be free. I feel more peace. Even though I still have occasional moments of bitterness, I'm getting better.

Insights and Scriptures to Get Better, Not Bitter
EVERYDAY APPLICATIONS

What I learned:

1. Forgiving the offense without addressing the impact of the offense and processing unhealthy emotions is not the complete work God wants me to do.

2. Anger is an emotion that signals that there is a problem. It's not bad or wrong, nor is it a tactic, method, or means to respond to the problem.

3. Unresolved anger leads to bitterness and resentment. These emotions result in an unforgiving heart and a negative and critical attitude.

4. Holding onto bitterness only hurts me.

5. My feelings, emotions, attitudes, thoughts, and behaviors are my property—they define who I am. I'm responsible for and must own them.

6. My healing is not dependent on anyone else. I regain power when I shift the responsibility of healing back to myself and away from those who have offended me.

7. God uses my experiences to shape me to be more like Jesus. My most challenging circumstances can be used to increase my empathy and give me an extra measure of perseverance, strength, and compassion toward others.

8. I must pray for God to help me see my difficulties from his perspective. Even hurtful experiences can teach me valuable lessons.

9. God's discipline will be carried out in his way and in his timing, not mine. God is always at work for my good. I need

to trust that he's at work in those who caused my wounds, just like he's at work in me.

10. After forgiveness and processing through my pain, a final step in healing is acceptance. Acceptance looks at my situation in a nonjudgmental way. To move forward, I must accept those difficult parts of my life, embrace them as part of my story, and move on to what lies ahead.

Scriptures that led me to these insights:

- "I have told you these things, so that in me you may have peace. In this world you will have trouble. But take heart! I have overcome the world." John 16:33

- Whoever is slow to anger has great understanding, but he who has a hasty temper exalts folly. (Proverbs 14:29 ESV)

- Good sense makes one slow to anger, and it is his glory to overlook an offense. (Proverbs 19:11 ESV)

- Everyone should be quick to listen, slow to speak and slow to become angry, because human anger does not produce the righteousness that God desires. (James 1:19-20)

- "In your anger do not sin": Do not let the sun go down while you are still angry, and do not give the devil a foothold. (Ephesians 4:26-27)

- Cease from anger, forsake wrath; do not fret—it only causes harm. (Psalm 37:8 NKJV)

- Watch out that no poisonous root of bitterness grows up to trouble you, corrupting many. (Hebrews 12:15 NLT)

- Get rid of all bitterness, rage, anger, harsh words, and slander, as well as all types of evil behavior. (Ephesians 4:31 NLT)

- If any of you lacks wisdom, let him ask God, who gives generously to all without reproach, and it will be given him. (James 1:5 ESV)

- And we know that in all things God works for the good of those who love him, who have been called according to his purpose. (Romans 8:28)

- Praise be to the God and Father of our Lord Jesus Christ, the Father of compassion and the God of all comfort, who comforts us in all our troubles, so that we can comfort those in any trouble with the comfort we ourselves receive from God. (2 Corinthians 1:3-4)

- Search me O God and know my heart, test me and know my anxious thoughts, see if there are any offensive ways in me, and lead me into your way everlasting. (Psalm 139:23-24)

Chapter 10

INSIGHT 7: BE CONTENT IN GOD'S ASSIGNMENTS

I felt like my life was on hold during my illnesses. Much of my time and mental capacity was spent trying to figure out the cause of my health issues. I'd think, *Once I get better, then I'll get more involved in something, or help someone, or be something more.* I often found myself frustrated with my circumstances. It felt like I wasn't making good use of my time or serving a greater purpose.

This happened over and over as I faced different health challenges. It seemed like I was staring at my own version of *Groundhog Day*.[1] I was discouraged and frustrated by my circumstances and felt like I'd never get out of this cycle. I was ready to be free, and I often wondered if I'd ever get out of this constant battle of discouragement and live a more purposeful life.

---

[1] Harold Ramis, dir. *Groundhog Day*. 1993; Columbia Pictures.

After my health began to improve following my hysterectomy, I thought I'd have a greater sense of purpose, but I found myself in another season when I was again frustrated and discouraged, feeling a lack of direction. And this time, I couldn't blame my health.

Although I was a working mother while raising Dylan and Tyler, I'd scaled back professional commitments a couple of years before Tyler's senior year to take full advantage of as much mom time as I could. I knew that season was coming to an end.

For twenty-five years, I had a 24/7 job as a mom while also working outside the home. Even when my kids were in their early teens, I had meals to prepare, activities to attend, volunteer work, and daily issues to resolve. Then, on August 17, 2017, Tyler went to college and I became an empty nester. I felt lost and without direction. Even though I experienced something similar when Dylan went off to school, this time there was no other child where I could turn my attention. My kids were grown up. I wrote in my journal that I felt like I had just gotten fired. Overnight, things changed, and I just wanted to be needed.

I cried out to God, saying, "I have all this wisdom I've gained as a mom. Please show me how I can use that wisdom now."

While I'd crafted a purpose statement a few years earlier, I hadn't nailed down the specifics. I knew I wanted to share my knowledge and experience with others, but I didn't know what specific knowledge or expertise I felt led to share, and I certainly didn't know with whom I was supposed to share it. Here I was, frustrated again and without a clear direction.

I'd already gone through such incredible spiritual growth and insight; wasn't I done yet? Did the Lord want to teach me more?

So I decided to figure out the "what" and "to whom" of that purpose statement, and events began to reveal pieces of this puzzle. As I was floundering around that fall after Tyler went to college, I decided to get involved in a women's Bible study at our church. During the first session, one of the leaders made a comment that I wrote in my Bible study guide: "Younger women want older women to chime in. To tell them what they know."

On that same day, an announcement was made about a women's discipleship program. Scripture in the book of Titus was referenced that calls older women to train younger women to live godly lives as wives, moms, and individuals (Titus 2:4-5). I wondered if this was the answer to my yearning.

I felt like the Bible verse in Titus was a directive to me. After the Bible study, I saw the director of the women's ministry, explained my situation, and told her I was interested in the discipleship program. I told her I wanted to take what was in my cup and pour it into someone else's. It was a passing conversation, but perhaps another puzzle piece was revealed.

A few weeks later, I reached out to her and asked to meet. I reiterated that I was interested in the discipleship program, and I shared that I was nervous and doubted my spiritual knowledge. She reassured me that I was ready to do this and told me that the women's discipleship team had paired me with a young woman after our previous conversation.

I was excited that they were at work even before I agreed to do it. What amazed me was how much the young woman and I had in common, including things the discipleship team didn't know. We were both raised Catholic, and we experienced the death of a loved one at a very young age. She was a young girl when she lost her mother, and I became a widow in my early twenties. Our pairing felt much like a match made in heaven.

We began meeting in January 2018. Our similar religious upbringing prepared me to pour into her biblical teachings and understanding at a pace that she could handle. We had deep spiritual conversations, and we discussed several professional and educational decisions and talked about preparations for her upcoming wedding in May that year. She was living a hectic and packed life, and I appreciated that she was making time for our new mentoring relationship.

Two days after her wedding, tragedy struck. She and her stepmom were involved in a canoeing accident. Her stepmom was killed, she was rescued, and the entire experience was incredibly traumatic. A time of celebration and excitement for her new marriage became a time of sorrow.

Only God knew what was in store for her when we started meeting earlier that year. He saw fit to connect us before that tragic situation, so when the crisis in her life hit, we could walk through it together. More than five years later, we continue to meet and experience new seasons with new jobs, new homes, and a growing family. Our friendship, and my role as her mentor, showed me my first glimpse of what became my new purpose.

God has put more women in my path to disciple—all different ages and walks of life. It's a blessing to pour what is in my cup into these other women. As I hear their triumphs and trials, I connect with them personally and meaningfully.

I now see how the puzzle pieces had come together to clarify my purpose statement—to help other women by sharing wisdom and knowledge that I've gained from my life experiences. As I share my stories, I'm led to tell all that God has done for me to encourage and help them in their journeys.

What started out as a season of frustration and discouragement now has purpose. I'm still needed, but in a different sense than with my children. With my clearly defined purpose, I hoped that these cycles of frustration and discouragement would come to an end.

I realized soon after that there was more to learn on my spiritual journey, and unless I learned to react to challenging situations differently, I'd continue to fall into these frustration and discouragement battles. My next experience would open my eyes to show me that I needed to see all my circumstances from a different perspective.

About a year into my mentoring role, the women's ministry leader asked if I'd be interested in speaking to the church staff during their weekly chapel. She wanted me to share my story of being an empty nester and how God redeemed that time of my life through the mentorship program.

Initially, I was both honored and excited. My pride got a big boost. But, as I read her request further, I saw that the staff was discussing topics from the book *Respectable Sins*[2] by Jerry Bridges. She was responsible for leading the discussion about discontentment— one of the "respectable" sins Bridges outlines in the book—and she thought my story as an empty nester was a real-life example.

I was stunned.

I'd never looked at my frustrations and dissatisfaction as an empty nester as a form of discontentment, much less a sin. Much like when Tim had first suggested to David that my health problems might have something to do with how I'd dealt—or failed to deal— with past trauma, my pride was hurt, and I was offended at first. After further thought, I figured God had some additional spiritual growth and insight in store for me, so I accepted her invitation and began to dive into this topic.

When I looked up the meaning of discontentment, the dictionary said "being dissatisfied with one's possessions, status, or situation." It was easy for me to understand how a person could be discontent over their possessions or status, but the word "situation" got my attention. I could see that my seasons of illness and even the start of my empty nest season were all situations where I found myself unhappy, frustrated, complaining, and dissatisfied, but was I discontent?

Heck, yeah, I was discontent. Who wouldn't be?

I immediately met with the women's ministry leader again and asked her to shed light on what is "respectable" sin and why discontentment is included. She explained that respectable sins (also referred to as "acceptable" sins) are subtle personal sins that we often tolerate in ourselves—and include selfishness, impatience, envy, jealousy, gossip, pride, and discontentment, among others. These may seem less serious compared to flagrant sin like murder, but in God's eyes they're still sinful behaviors.

---

[2] Jerry Bridges, *Respectable Sins* (Colorado Springs: NavPress, 1973)

Regarding discontentment, regardless of our circumstances, it's our response to those circumstances that determines if we're discontent. To be clear, it's not the circumstance that is in question here, but how we respond. Our dissatisfaction, frustration and even bitterness with our circumstances—often directed at God—show that we don't trust God's will for our lives, and we don't trust that he is working things out for our good or trust his timing.

That was a tough pill to swallow. I mean, I can understand that discontentment with our possessions and status could be considered sinful. But what about the difficult circumstances I endured all those years? The ongoing dissatisfaction and unhappiness I experienced during that season felt justified to me.

The hard truth is God is sovereign over all things and he uses our circumstances for his glory and our good. My view of my circumstances is very limited, whereas God's view is much bigger. Psalm 139:16 says, "…all the days ordained for me were written in your book before one of them came to be." Since God has a much bigger picture of my life, he has purpose for it all and I have to trust God is at work for my good, even if it doesn't look that way in the short term. I have to trust he knows what's best for me and accept that his ways and timing could be completely different from mine.

God understands that we can become weary and weak, and he wants us to come to him so he can renew our strength and increase our ability to persevere (Isaiah 40:29). But, as we pray for healing and relief, and take positive steps toward changing or improving our circumstances, we do it with a heart of acceptance that God knows best—with an attitude of courage and perseverance.

I'm not implying that in difficult circumstances we're supposed to ignore our situation, put a smile on our face, and pretend all is well. But, if God is in control, sovereign over all my circumstances and has some greater purpose in them, then I want to respond differently and understand how to do that.

This realization was eye-opening for me. If this was true, looking over my life, I experienced discontentment over and over again. I needed to get a handle on this. Don't we all struggle with discontentment and frustration when we're in difficult seasons of life? Wouldn't we all just as soon be in a better place?

I began to pray that God would give me his perspective on this. I wanted to recognize and quickly overcome discontentment when it came knocking at my door and reframe my thinking. I may not prevent these initial feelings the next time I'm in an unpleasant situation, but I think that's part of our human instinct that we wrestle with on this side of heaven. But I want to see my circumstances differently and prevent that discontentment from making me angry, disappointed, or bitter. I knew I needed to shift my thinking and get my mind right about this.

Then it hit me—a new way of seeing *all* my circumstances. God is sovereign and all-knowing, and he already has a plan for me. Since that's true, then I should consider all my circumstances as his *assignments*. Assignments made sense to me. They felt purposeful, like a job or a task.

Not all jobs are pleasant, but I can still give it my best. When I began to come to terms with that, I realized I needed to view my circumstance as something God has assigned me to do, and to faithfully react to them with purpose and intentionality.

The question is how we look at each assignment, even if it's challenging, and be content no matter the situation—like the Apostle Paul did—without all the frustration, discouragement, and discontentment that I experienced repeatedly.

After much thought, prayer, and Bible study, God revealed some things that I'm trying to implement in my life now. These are six questions and lessons I lean on whenever I find myself in any assignment—especially when those familiar feelings of discontentment or frustration are knocking at my door.

First, how can I have a more purposeful view of my circumstances?

The apostle Paul said his imprisonment served to advance the gospel—that his situation became clear to everyone around him that he was in chains for Christ (Philippians 1:12). While he was in prison, his actions served as a testimony to others to believe in Christ and spur others to share the gospel. Paul had every reason to want out of his circumstances, but rather than be discontent, Paul saw his imprisonment as an assignment with a greater purpose.

If Paul saw the greater purpose of his circumstances, can we do the same? Like him, we can take a broader view of our circumstances and see that our attitudes and actions in our assignment can be a testament to Christ in us as well. We can be faithful in our circumstances, no matter how easy or hard—handling them in a way that points others to Christ.

Second, how can I learn to be content regardless of my circumstances?

Paul says in Philippians that he *learned* to be content. Paul led a life filled with many challenges and successes. He was beaten, flogged, shipwrecked, imprisoned, sick, threatened, and more. Before that, he was an affluent Jew. He had it all, and then he had nothing, and he said, "I have learned the secret of being content whatever the situation" (Philippians 4:12).

Do you know what the secret was? Paul said he learned to be content in whatever circumstance he faced because Christ gave him the strength to do so through the Holy Spirit inside of him (Philippians 4:13). It was a process.

Perhaps Paul suffered from discontentment early on in his journey. Who knows? But I know his success wasn't because of his own strength. Christ within him gave him the power to overcome his discontentment and frustrations.

We can use the same strength through the Holy Spirit to defeat our own discontentment and frustrations.

Third, how can I trust that God is at work even if I don't see anything?

It's imperative to remind ourselves that God is *always* at work for our good (Romans 8:28), and his ways and his timing are often different from ours (Isaiah 55:8). Even when our circumstance is challenging, we have to remind ourselves that God is at work even when we don't see it.

I know you may be in circumstances where the last thing you feel is that God is anywhere near, much less doing anything good. I get that, and I've felt that too. But this is where you get to stand on his Word confidently—to stand even when your flesh doesn't want to, to *believe him* and his word.

Fourth, how can I surrender my control, especially when I don't see God's hand yet?

When we let go of our control, we can let God lead. Remember in Psalm 23, David proclaims that the Lord is his shepherd—that we're to be like sheep and let God lead us. God, our shepherd, knows best.

Honestly, sometimes what is most needed is to get out of the way—to surrender to his care. I know I tend to jump in and try to fix things before I ever go to God with them, but isn't that like saying that I have more faith in my own abilities than in God's abilities? I hate admitting that's how I act in the heat of the moment, but I catch myself doing just that. God's abilities are far greater than my own, and I have to trust him and submit to him, knowing he'll direct my path (Proverbs 3:5-6).

Fifth, how can I fight my discontentment in my current assignment?

I've realized I have to develop expectant endurance. The truth of the matter is, it's not the easy parts of life that strengthen our character, it's the difficult circumstances and how we deal with them that mold us. Our struggles build our endurance and perseverance. They grow our character and mature our faith (Romans 5:3-4 ESV). If you can pause long enough to see that whatever you're going through can provide you with ways to learn and grow, then you can experience hope in an otherwise hopeless situation and fight off discontentment. I know it's cliché, but if God brings you to it, be confident he'll bring you through it.

Sixth, what is God's wisdom for what I can *do* throughout the entire process—minute by minute?

This one is hard—not that the other five are easy—because so often, we act like human doings and not human beings. But God wants us to pray continually and give thanks in all our circumstances (1 Thessalonians 5:17-18).

I know the edict to pray continually and to give thanks in all situations can be hard to fathom. I thought that as well until my perspective shifted.

We aren't giving thanks for the circumstance. Instead, we're giving thanks that God is with us. For that, I'm eternally grateful. Can you imagine your most challenging assignments without *him*?

We know that in this life, there will be trouble (John 16:33). But, if life is a series of assignments, then shouldn't we consider that our assignments are found both in life's good times and the difficult ones? I don't know about you, but I'd like to handle myself in each of my assignments (good and bad) in a way that's pleasing to God and trusting him, rather than being frustrated and discontent all the time.

These are all good reminders to shift my heart from discontentment to a spirit of trust. When the storm is swelling and my mind is going ninety to nothing, these simple truths help center me to where I'm looking up to God to strengthen me instead of looking to myself.

I found myself lingering on this chapter because of my discontentment even during this book writing process. I've been wrestling with how long it's taken (more than three years) and concerned with people's reactions to my story—doubting that I should even continue. So, as I edited this chapter, I found these truths to be powerful reminders even in my current circumstance.

Maybe God was trying to reteach a lesson to me in the middle of this journey, too.

Insights and Scriptures to Be Content in God's Assignments
EVERYDAY APPLICATIONS

What I learned:

1. Discontentment means "being dissatisfied with one's possessions, status, or situation."

2. From a biblical perspective, being discontent or dissatisfied with my circumstances (or possessions or status) shows that I don't trust God's will for my life and that I believe I know what's best instead of him.

3. "Respectable" sins, also referred to as "acceptable" sins, are subtle sinful behaviors I tolerate in myself. These may seem minor, but in God's eyes they are a sin, and sin is sin. Discontentment is a type of acceptable sin—as are selfishness, impatience, envy, jealousy, and pride, gossip, among others.

4. Consider all circumstances and seasons I find myself in as assignments from God. Assignments are purposeful.

5. Take a broader view of my assignments. My attitudes and actions in all my assignments can be a testament to Christ in us.

6. Learn contentment. If it doesn't come naturally, then depend on strength from the Holy Spirit within to handle my assignments.

7. Trust that God is always at work for my good. His ways and his timing may not be the same as mine.

8. Develop my endurance muscle, knowing that it produces character and hope.

9. Pray my way through a season of discontentment continuously, and be thankful that God is always with me.

Scriptures that led to these insights:

- Then they can urge the younger women to love their husbands and children, to be self-controlled and pure, to be busy at home, to be kind, and to be subject to their husbands, so that no one will malign the word of God. (Titus 2:4-5)

- Your eyes saw my unformed body; all the days ordained for me were written in your book before one of them came to be. (Psalm 139:16)

- He gives strength to the weary and increases the power of the weak. Even youth grow tired and weary, and young men stumble and fall; but those who hope in the Lord will renew their strength. (Isaiah 40:29-31)

- I want you to know, brothers, that what has happened to me has really served to advance the gospel. (Philippians 1:12)

- I know what it is to be in need, and I know what it is to have plenty. I have learned the secret of being content in any and every situation, whether well fed or hungry, whether living in plenty or in want. (Philippians 4:12)

- I can do all things through Christ who gives me strength. (Philippians 4:13)

- And we know that in all things God works for the good of those who love him, who have been called according to his purpose. (Romans 8:28)

- "For my thoughts are not your thoughts, neither are your ways my ways," declares the Lord. (Isaiah 55:8)

- Trust in the Lord with all your heart, and do not lean on your own understanding. In all your ways submit to him, and he will make your paths straight. (Proverbs 3:5-6)

- Not only that, but we rejoice in our sufferings, knowing that suffering produces endurance, and endurance produces character, and character produces hope. (Romans 5:3-4 ESV)

- Pray continually, give thanks in all circumstances; for this is God's will for you in Christ Jesus. (1 Thessalonians 5:17-18)

- I have told you these things, so that in me you may have peace. In this world you will have trouble. But take heart! I have overcome the world. (John 16:33)

Chapter 11

INSIGHT 8: ADOPT AN ABUNDANCE MINDSET

In 2017, I began using the "one word" technique to give focus to my year. Instead of making a list of resolutions that I often fail to achieve, the idea is to prayerfully come up with one word that represents the main area I want to focus on that year. In 2018, I chose the word brave. I felt I had been brave through my extended physical health battle, and I wanted to be brave going forward. Little did I know that it would take on an entirely different meaning than I could've imagined.

That fall, I received an invitation to a ceremony commemorating the thirty-fifth anniversary of the terrorist attack in Beirut. I'd never attended the annual event. In fact, I hadn't been back to Camp Lejeune since I moved away in 1984. The thought of going back—of seeing John's name etched on the memorial wall along with the names of the others lost in the attack—had always filled me with fear of experiencing the pain, grief, loss, and trauma all over again. As time rolled by, the fear seemed to get more significant, dark, and daunting.

As he'd done in previous years, David gently asked if I thought it was time to attend the ceremony. Each time he asked, I put him off by saying that I needed to think more about it. On October 5— our twenty-seventh wedding anniversary—David brought it up one last time. He knew we needed to make travel arrangements if we were going.

This time I gave him a definitive answer: No. I'd had my fair share of healing, and I thought I'd done enough, that I'd been through enough. I felt good where I was, where God had led me. I didn't make the decision lightly, we even prayed about it, and I was comfortable with my answer.

The following day, I woke up earlier than David and went out to the family room to have my coffee and quiet time. It was unusual that David hadn't already been awake since he typically wakes up before me. So I settled in with my coffee and sat on the sofa. I figured I'd do a quick email check before starting my quiet time. As I scanned my email, one subject line caught my attention: "White House Invitation."

What?

The President

requests the pleasure of your company

at a reception commemorating the

35th Anniversary of the

Attack on the Beirut Barracks

to be held at

The White House

on Thursday, October 25, 2018

at six o'clock

Business Attire   *Southeast Entrance*

I was stunned. Never in my wildest dreams had I thought this would happen. For reasons that still puzzle me, the Beirut bombing had been ignored by those in power and swept under the rug for decades. And, because of this, it was forgotten by the media and the public. When the purpose of this mission was to be a presence of peace instead of a position of combat, we hadn't anticipated nor prepared for an enemy that was willing to commit suicide to support their cause. Although some say we were unprepared for such a heinous act, from my seat, it sure seemed like our hands were tied.

The attack on the Beirut barracks was the largest non-nuclear explosion the world had seen before 9/11, killing 241 servicemen and starting the war on terrorism. Yet each year, October 23 comes and goes without the media adequately recognizing it—much less those lost and the families that survived. The event had been ignored by most presidents, aside from Ronald Reagan's involvement the year it happened—until now.

I thought about my conversation with David the night before. I'd been emphatic about my decision not to go to Camp Lejeune. But now what? I sat there staring at the email. How could I ignore an opportunity to personally hear from the leaders of our country concerning this tragic event? However, I realized that if I considered going to the White House, I'd also have to go back to Camp Lejeune.

When David woke up, he came into the family room and asked me what I was up to.

I showed him the email with the invitation and said, "I guess God figured he'd have to get the president of the United States to invite me to the White House for me to face my fears and go back to where this all started."

David stood there in shock. He asked me what I was thinking. I shared my thoughts about this unexpected invitation and the fact that I didn't think I should attend this without also going back to North Carolina. Then I asked him to go with me, and David agreed.

The decision was made.

I was overcome with fear, and I shared all my feelings with

David. Scared. Uncertain. Worried. Here we go again. All those feelings I was so good at stuffing started overwhelming me, and I heard all kinds of lies in my head. I couldn't stop the spiral.

David's response changed the trajectory of this trip for me and even for my life going forward. "Theresa, maybe think of this from an abundance mindset instead of scarcity."

I asked him for more details. He explained that he was struggling with some business decisions, and realized that in the past, his choices were often based on fear. He found himself making decisions based on all the possible bad things that could happen rather than good ones. Recently, he read about changing to an abundance mindset and expecting good instead of bad. Rather than expecting scarcity he was learning to expect abundance and make decisions based on that mentality.

For me, that meant expecting that God had good intentions here. He wanted to use this trip and these ceremonies to do something good. I liked what David was saying, but I wasn't totally on board yet. I'm a processor, and I needed to let that sink in. I was fighting back old familiar fears that something bad would happen. So, while writing in my journal that morning, I asked myself some questions.

"Is God out to get me?" *No.*

"Does he have plans for me, plans to prosper me and not to harm me?" *Yes.*

"Is God at work here? And is it for my good?" *Yes. He's always at work for my good.*

"WWJD?" (What would Jesus do?) *I think he'd go!*

So I told David I was all in. Then I decided to focus on some critical thoughts for this trip. To me, they were game-changers.

First, no more fear.

It was time to more fully embrace my 2018 word: brave. That word was very fitting, wasn't it? I decided that no matter what we did, where we went, or who we saw, I wasn't going to give in to my fears. That I was going to be brave. That God was using this experience for my good.

Second, remember.

Now that I was willing to return, I wanted to remember everything I'd stuffed about this event. The memories were way back in the recesses of my mind, buried deep, and since they were buried, I had a hard time remembering anything. I wanted to remember all about the Marine Corps, about the specifics of John's deployment, about the people deployed with him, and even become familiar again with Marine Corps acronyms, ranks, and chains of command.

Third, reconnect.

I wanted to reconnect with someone who knew John and knew me. You see, since I'd disconnected myself from this part of my life for so long, I couldn't remember anyone, and thirty-five years can make us all look different, too. How would I recognize anyone? They'd have to remember me, and that was a tall order. I was twenty-three at the time, and so much had happened since that awful attack. People change. I'd changed.

With my newfound abundance mindset, we began making our plans. We were asked to correspond with the social secretary of the White House.

How cool is that?

This was real. I was going on the trip that I had been avoiding for practically all of my adult life. I was so grateful that David would be by my side.

A few days after I made the conscious decision to remember everything I could, I knew it was time to open and unpack the box of John's personal things that I so painfully packed and sealed in 1983. That box included letters, medals, awards, and correspondences, but it also carried the emotions and pain from that horrific experience. For more than three decades I'd been too afraid to open it and face all that was inside. I knew it was time to face those fears and let the memories and emotions flow.

I went to our storage room upstairs, found the box, and carried it to our family room. I sat on the floor, unsealed it, took out each item, and spread the contents all around me. Since I was still in shock when I originally packed that box decades earlier, it felt like I was looking at some of these things for the first time.

It blew my mind.

There were letters from John that he wrote while he was in Beirut, a letter from President Reagan offering his condolences, and letters from various congressmen, diplomats, college friends, hometown friends, and Marines.

I found medals that John was awarded, including the Purple Heart and the Navy Commendation Medal. There was a box of military personal items like pins and insignia for John's rank, badges, and ribbons. I kept a pocket watch that I'd given him on a special occasion.

I even found the program from the memorial service in North Carolina where President Reagan and the first lady were present. For all these years I'd wondered if the event was a memory or something I'd dreamed, and seeing that piece of paper confirmed that it had actually happened, and I was there.

As you can imagine, I cried many healing tears as I carefully reviewed the contents. I was surrounded by historical artifacts that were fitting for a museum like the Smithsonian Institution, and I felt a sense of respect and pride as I looked over the keepsakes of a hero's life.

I'd finally unpacked the box and felt like it was another step in unpacking all the emotions that I had stuffed so long ago.

On October 22, we flew to Jacksonville, home of Camp Lejeune, in time to go to the Beirut Memorial by ourselves. We arrived as the sun was setting. It was so serene. The memorial is incredible, made of two granite walls. One wall is engraved with the names of everyone killed in this attack, including John's. The second wall carries the inscription, "They Came in Peace," which represents their purpose of being a peaceful presence in a war-torn Lebanon. In the middle stands a bronze statue of a Marine. We soaked this all in; it was such a quiet and peaceful time.

When we arrived at the sunrise service the next day, the place was already brimming with nearly 1,000 people. We parked and rushed to the memorial. I heard an announcement for volunteers to read out loud the names on the wall during the ceremony. They also said that anyone who wanted to speak a specific name could do so and come forward. It was go time. No time to be afraid. I went right up front and told them I wanted to say John's name.

The ceremony was held by candlelight. Imagine 1,000 people, all with candles, surrounding this memorial. A marine officer who was present during the bombing opened the ceremony. He talked about a Native American tradition where warriors would gather annually and speak out the names of those killed in battle, a tradition that had been adopted in this particular ceremony. So one-by-one each of the 241 names etched on that wall was recited. Just before my time to announce John's name, my heart was pounding in my ears.

I said, "John N. Boyett, USMC," at the top of my lungs. It felt like all the pent-up fear escaped me.

At 6:22 a.m., the exact same time the bombing took place thirty-five years earlier, another marine recounted the story of the bombing. When the story was told, the memories flooded my mind. Although it was emotional, it was beautiful as well. What a meaningful way to honor those who lost their lives, to state their names out loud and give those fallen heroes a voice.

When the service ended, we went back to the hotel to eat breakfast and prepare for another ceremony later that morning. Once again, there were tons of people. Lots of traffic. Parking lots were full. I was tense, just wanting to get seated. I remember feeling out of place, not knowing what to expect, and not knowing anyone. I kept hearing the lies of the enemy say to me, "You're a coward.

Aren't you ashamed of yourself for not coming back until now?" I felt like everyone was staring at me and thinking that too, but I kept reminding myself of my one word, *brave*, and I held on to my abundance mindset. I trusted God and prayed for him to lead the way.

We had been told there was special seating for the family members of those killed, so David and I headed in that direction. We sat beside a man and his wife. The man's younger brother was also killed. We talked, and I felt led to explain to his wife that I hadn't been back since it happened. She could tell I was timid and uncertain.

"It takes everyone in their own time to come back," she said. "Some more time than others."

What a thoughtful thing to say to make me feel at ease. To dispel any fear that I might be battling and quiet my thoughts.

The ceremony commenced with guest speakers, including the mayor of Jacksonville, the current commandant of the Marine Corps, and Gen. Alfred M. Gray, who was instrumental in the activities after the bombing. Each of them recalled the event. They reminded the crowd of the bravery of those who lost their lives and of their honor and love of this country. They played taps before the end of the ceremony along with a twenty-one gun salute to honor those killed.[1]

That's when I lost it—I was immediately taken back to John's funeral. It was like it was happening all over again.

Unexpectedly, the woman who comforted me earlier wrapped her arms around me and held me. She knew my hurt and the pain. She was familiar with it. What an incredible show of love from a complete stranger.

When the ceremony ended, she turned to me, and without hesitation, she said, "Welcome home, Theresa. We've missed you."

---

[1] "Beirut Memorial Observance 2018." Filmed October 23, 2018, in Jacksonville, NC. Jacksonville NC video on YouTube 1:18:06. https://www.youtube.com/watch?v=NjoitgPj1kQ.

Wow.

There were no words for the gratitude I felt for this woman and the pride and honor I felt for the Marine Corps. It was indeed an emotional time and a time of further healing.

After the ceremony, I stood alone at the wall, reflecting on the morning's events. I silently had a little prayer conversation with God, thanking him for leading me back to North Carolina and for the couple who sat next to us. Thanking him for giving me the courage to be brave. Thanking him for David being with me. It was then that I distinctly felt the Lord gently whispering, "See, Theresa, you never had anything to fear. I've always been with you and patiently waiting for you to come back."

He was so right.

After that, we loaded up the car and headed to Washington, DC, and I was totally pumped thinking about what else the Lord may have in store. David and I even decided to take a short side trip to Wilmington, where I attended college. I finished my degree less than two months after the bombing, but I didn't attend my graduation, nor had I returned since. It was just another part of my history that I'd packed away.

I was so glad I returned. The campus had grown since I was there in 1983, but there were several familiar buildings. David and I walked around the beautiful campus, and I showed him where my business classes took place and talked about some of my favorite courses and professors. It felt so good to show him that part of my life, just like we'd done so many times at the University of Arkansas, where he attended.

After spending a couple hours there, we headed on to Washington for the second leg of our trip. On the drive, David asked me how I felt about the trip so far. I told him what I felt the Lord had put on my heart during my reflection at the wall. I told him I was excited that two of my three prayers were being answered. First, not to fear, and, second, to remember things. I told him I was also disappointed that I didn't see anyone who knew John or me at the memorial service.

David reminded me, "Well, it's not over yet. God still has time." And that set the tone for what was next.

Later that evening, I reached out to my nephew Blake, who'd served in the Marine Corps. I told him what I was doing and that I wanted help recalling some details about the military. I asked him to explain the organization of the Corps, like squadrons, platoons, and battalions, and remind me of the different ranks. Later that night, he texted me and said he found a group on Facebook, Beirut Memorial OnLine. He suggested I join the group so that maybe I could get more of my questions answered.

I joined the group that evening, posted a picture of John in uniform, and asked if anyone on the site knew him. The page flooded with comments from former marines who'd worked for him and even fellow officers. I also learned more about others killed in his company.

I can't tell you how it felt to have information again. I got more details from Facebook thirty-five years later than I had when the bombing happened. Without social media, cell phones, or laptops, information was incredibly scarce, but thanks to modern technology I was beginning to feel reconnected.

The next day, October 25, David had to do some work in the hotel, so I made a point of journaling about our trip. Getting ready for the event was exciting, but I was crazy nervous. I felt that God would show up somehow, and I wanted to make sure I soaked it all in.

Going to the White House was amazing. Everyone we encountered seemed to be a little timid and quiet, not saying much to each other as we passed through several high-security checkpoints. And, as only God does, he gave us a little comic relief. David showed one of the guards his driver's license.

The guard took a look and said, "Would you be David Lee Roth from Van Halen?"

Everyone around had a good laugh. It was just the thing we all needed to relax, and we all chatted amongst ourselves from that point on.

As I stood there, I recalled my nephew saying that since John was a first lieutenant, he might have been the executive officer—known as XO—of his company. He also recommended that I be on the lookout for anyone else who might hold that same position for another company, that they more than likely would know John. So my antennae went up when I heard a man a few people ahead of us remark that he was the XO for Charlie Company.

Did he know John?

Once we were all through security, I introduced myself to the man, told him I overheard him introducing himself, and asked if he might have known John. And he did. He told me John was an outstanding leader, a favorite among his peers and men, and did an exceptional job. I was ecstatic to meet someone who remembered John! My third prayer had just been answered—and God wasn't done.

Once we passed all the security checks, we were told that we could explore the White House. We visited rooms lined with books and famous portraits of former presidents and their families displayed along the hallways. David and I were mesmerized by it all. Knowing that former presidents and statesmen had also walked these floors made it feel like hallowed ground.

As we wandered from room to room, I saw a woman taking pictures of a couple and thought to myself, *what a great idea to capture this moment with David.* So I asked her if she'd do the same for us, and David and I now have a wonderful photo of the two of us that we'll always cherish.

After the woman took our picture, she walked over to a gentleman who looked familiar to me. He was much younger, but he reminded me of someone I knew. It was just a passing moment, a quick observation, and I didn't say anything to him. I continued to pray that the Lord would lead me through the evening.

From there, we were told to go to the West Wing for the commemoration ceremony. We were still uncertain exactly what this ceremony would entail, so David asked a marine who handed us a program what was about to happen.

"The president will arrive in about fifteen minutes, along with several other dignitaries, to address everyone present," the marine said. "After that, food and drinks will be available, the Marine Corps Orchestra will perform, and you all are invited to mingle the next couple of hours."

Is this for real?

At first, I was a bit disappointed because many of the seats up close were already taken. But I said a quick prayer for God to lead us to exactly where he wanted us to sit, which turned out to be on the left side of where President Trump would enter. As we looked around, we saw loads of cameras, members of the media, security, and other guests like us who were family members or survivors. As I looked around, I kept wondering if anyone knew John—or perhaps even someone who knew me.

Not long after we were seated, a man and woman in wheelchairs were positioned beside David. I recognized the man, even thirty-five years later, as John's commanding officer, Lt. Col. Larry Gerlach. He was a great leader and kind to John. He had promoted John to first lieutenant in 1982. I wanted to make sure that I spoke to him after the ceremony.

I also saw General Gray, who had spoken at the morning ceremony in North Carolina. Although not in Beirut during the bombing, General Gray played a crucial role in changing Marine policies to incorporate new rules of engagement for terrorist events. So many people held him in high regard, and I wanted to make sure I introduced myself to him, as well. As I continued to glance over the crowd, I realized that the woman who took our picture and the man who looked oddly familiar to me were sitting behind us. Again, I wasn't sure there was any connection, but I made a mental note.

Before I had too much time to get lost in my thoughts, "Hail to the Chief" began to play, and in walked President Donald Trump.

Those present for this ceremony let out a huge round of applause. Never before had a president done anything this significant to publicly lift up those who survived this tragic event, nor had any of them honored those who lost their lives and the families left behind. Thirty-five years of our loved ones being forgotten was no more. We were proud and thankful for this kind gesture that our government, and especially our president, made.

President Trump introduced additional dignitaries, and it was a who's who of government representatives that included the secretary of state, the secretary of defense, the secretary of the Navy, the chairman of the Joint Chiefs of Staff, the Army chief of staff, the commandant of the Marine Corps, the commandant of the Coast Guard, the White House chief of staff, and several more. The enormity of this event set in at that point. To have so many dignitaries along with President Trump in person at this ceremony was monumental.

Whether you're a fan of Trump or not doesn't matter. So much has happened politically and in our country since I made that trip in 2018, but regardless of my political views, I was deeply moved by Trump's presence and heartfelt words. He reassured the audience that those who were lost were not forgotten and that they played a critical role in our country's history and for our freedom.

President Trump then asked those who survived to stand, and the room erupted with applause. He followed with a request for family members to stand representing those who made the ultimate sacrifice. As I stood, I felt honored to stand for John and receive the gratitude of our country for his sacrifice.

The president said, "Today, we pay tribute to the heroes you knew and loved. We grieve and mourn by your side. And we honor the immortal sacrifice of 241 heroes who gave their lives for our freedom."[2]

---

[2] "President Trump Delivers Remarks at the 35th Anniversary of the Attack on Beirut Barracks." Filmed October 25, 2018, in Washington, DC. Trump White House Archived video on YouTube 24:08. https://www.youtube.com/watch?v=cvsiBFIPSWI&t=12s (5:29-5:44).

I appreciated his comments.

I was equally moved when he said, "Each of these heroes died as they lived: as noble warriors—they were warriors—whose hearts were filled with courage and whose souls were rich with love. The United States Marines are often the first to deploy, the first into danger, and the first to fight. And, on that morning thirty-five years ago, they were among the very first to give their lives in the battle against radical Islamic terrorism—the battle that we are winning and we will win."[3]

As the ceremony closed, I walked toward Lieutenant Colonel Gerlach to reintroduce myself and remind him of John. After a kind exchange with him, I found General Gray and proceeded to introduce myself and tell him about John as well. Then I found myself face to face with that young man who looked oddly familiar.

Here you go, Theresa, no fear, just ask him who he is.

I didn't really know what else to say, so I asked if he was a survivor.

He smiled and said, "No, but my father was killed in Beirut."

I asked his father's name.

"My father was Dr. John Hudson," he said.

It took my breath away. I *knew* his Dad. "My husband was John Boyett, and we knew your dad," I said.

From behind this young man, the woman who had taken that photo earlier in the evening turned around. "Theresa, where have you been?" she said. "I've been looking for you for thirty-five years!"

I stood there in utter shock.

Someone knew John, *and* someone knew *me!* The woman behind the camera was Lisa Hudson, John Hudson's wife. We couldn't

---

[3] "President Trump Delivers Remarks at the 35th Anniversary of the Attack on Beirut Barracks." Filmed October 25, 2018, in Washington, DC. Trump White House Archived video on YouTube 24:08. https://www.youtube.com/watch?v=cvsiBFIPSWI&t=12s (8:40-9:14).

believe what had just happened. Memories flooded back. Lisa's husband was a Navy doctor. She and I had met at the Officers' Wives Club in 1982. She was also from Georgia, and that connection had made us immediate friends.

Three months before our husbands deployed, Lisa had given birth to a baby boy, and that baby boy was now the man standing in front of me. Lisa had moved back to Georgia to stay with her parents while her husband was overseas. We continued to keep in touch while the guys were gone until a few months after the bombing. But then, when I ran from this tragedy, I ran from her as well.

During that short reunion, Lisa reminded me that we were actually talking on the phone the night of the bombing just after midnight. Unbeknownst to us, we were on the phone with each other when this bombing actually occurred.

She also reminded me that she'd visited me at my parents' home in Albany in December 1983 and stayed for a couple of days. My memory about that was still fuzzy, but a few months after our trip to DC, my mom found a photo that my dad had taken of Lisa and me in my parents' living room during her visit. I was so glad to be reconnected with her, and I was so happy that she knew all those details to fill in the holes of my memory.

Yes, God was answering my prayers in mighty ways.

I explained to Lisa that this tragedy was just too much for me, and that the reason she couldn't find me was that I ran from everyone and moved to Atlanta to create a new reality.

We all were escorted out of the White House a couple of hours after the ceremony and reception. I was on a high of sorts, and David and I decided to go to Old Ebbitt Grill, a storied DC restaurant we'd been to years before, to reminisce about the life-changing evening.

There is no doubt that God had gone before me and paved the way for each of my three prayers to be answered. The fear that had bound me up and prevented me from returning to North Carolina and visiting the Beirut Memorial had vanished. In its place was a sense of God's heavenly hand that had so gently and patiently guided and directed me to make this trip.

My desire to remember and learn more about this event opened the floodgates. I more clearly understood what happened, who was affected, and how. And the Lord took my last request to see someone with a personal connection to John and me and blessed me beyond my imagination. An old friend who understands the living hell I went through is now my friend once again.

Yes, God was always at work for my good. The moment I decided to change my mindset from fear and scarcity to an attitude of abundance and goodness, I began to see God's mighty work on my life.

I'd created much of my mess. I was the one who stuffed my fears and pain. I was the one who ran from it all, but God waited so patiently for me. Then, when I took a chance and put my fears aside, he blessed me with these answered prayers beyond anything I could've hoped for.

In retrospect, I realized fear is a force to reckon with. It prevents abundance in life and is *not* from God. Scriptures remind us that God doesn't give us a spirit of fear but a spirit of power, love, and a sound mind (2 Timothy 1:7).

So, if God doesn't give us this spirit of fear, then who does? Yep, the enemy, the devil himself. You have a choice to make when fear comes knocking at your door. Are you going to be enslaved to it? Are you going to avoid doing things because of fear and react to something out of the fear of the unknown? Or are you going to believe the teachings of Jesus, who reminds us that he's given us a different kind of spirit—one of power and love and *not* of fear?

It's not a mistake that "do not be afraid" is mentioned hundreds of times in the Bible. God knows fear is something we battle, and his Word reassures us repeatedly. But we have to believe what he says and choose goodness over fear.

I'd let the enemy rob me of the blessings that God wanted to show me all those years—of the healing he wanted to provide and the prayers he wanted to answer. But I realized I had to make that first step. I had to set my fears aside and know that fear isn't from him, to believe God's promises for me.

So how can we transition from a mindset of fear and scarcity to an attitude of abundance and goodness? Change your mind. Change your thinking habits. Change your knee-jerk reactions.

There is a proverb that says, "As he thinks in his heart, so is he" (Proverbs 23:7 NKJV). If you think fear, you'll feel fear, and there is scientific evidence to support this, as well.

In her book *Switch On Your Brain*,[4] cognitive neuroscientist Dr. Caroline Leaf talks about the study of quantum physics. She explains that your mind controls your brain and, in turn, controls your body. So whatever your mind focuses on, your brain adapts and uses that information to determine how you feel and think. All that says to me is that I'd better get my mind under control so that my thoughts, feelings, and even actions lean more toward a positive outcome.

So how did I get my mind right, and how can you do the same? I implemented some helpful strategies.

My first strategy was to understand my fear before dealing with it.

I learned to recognize fear for what it is and think about where it's coming from. I realize there is healthy fear—like fear of running into a burning building or touching a hot stove. That's good fear, and it prevents me from potentially hurting myself. But not all fear is considered good. When we experience the emotion of fear, we have to observe it and ask ourselves if this is fear to protect us from danger, or is this fear hurting our well-being, health, relationships, or future in any way? If it's the latter, then more than likely that fear is not from God. So sharpen your awareness of the kind of fear you're experiencing. Pause as you feel it, and determine what kind of fear it is.

---

[4] Caroline Leaf, *Switch On Your Brain: The Key to Peak Happiness, Thinking, and Health* (Grand Rapids: Barker Books, 2013).

The second strategy I learned was to choose to listen to something else.

When I see that fear is harmful and hurting me, then I actively *choose not* to listen to it. These fears include catastrophic thoughts, worrisome thoughts, unrealistic thoughts, and thoughts of condemnation, just to name a few. Scripture tells us in 2 Corinthians 10:5 to "take captive every thought and make it obedient to Christ." I refer to that Bible verse often when my mind starts racing with fear and all the negative possibilities of a situation. When I get on a roll, my negative thoughts can get the best of me, but as this verse advises, I have to take these thoughts captive, to dispute them, to realize they're false. I literally interrupt the thought patterns with the Scripture above and replace them with God's truth.

One exercise I've practiced is to journal about the fear. Write it down. Getting it out of my head and on paper is helpful. Then I take it one step further. Once I write it down, I refute that fear-based thought with God's truth. I write down why that fear is unreasonable, unrealistic, or harmful. I even say it out loud.

Your brain needs to see and hear truthful thinking to refute those fearful thoughts. When you do that, it's incredible how quickly destructive thinking stops. The fear dissipates, and you start thinking clearly again. Other times, it happens less quickly, and if you have to, you can repeat that process over and over again.

The third strategy is to expect *good*.

Sometime in my life, someone told me not to expect anything good to happen to me. That way, I'm never disappointed when life deals me a bad hand. I'm not sure when it arrived or who it came from, but that message dug itself in deep, and I've had my share of hard knocks, so that thinking was pretty easy to adopt. But now I realize what a dismal and hopeless way that is to live. Never expecting good, never thinking that good things will happen, that sure seems hopeless to me. And I don't want to live with that mindset anymore.

Looking back, I was expecting something terrible to happen to me. Funny how I had a better outlook on life for everyone else. That's how Satan wants me to live—to fill my mind with all the "what ifs" before they ever even happen. A dear friend, Lisa Ogle, once told me: don't borrow trouble. That advice has stuck with me. When I expect bad things to happen, I'm borrowing trouble before it ever occurs. That's ridiculous. Don't do it. That's a scarcity mindset.

Proverbs 15:15 (NLT) speaks directly to this: "For the despondent, every day brings trouble; for the happy heart, life is a continual feast." I was letting fear rule my life instead of my faith in God. God is good—everything about him. I was living my life as if he was good to everyone *except* me, and that's a lie. So, just like I did when the invitation to the White House showed up, now I choose to expect good and abundance *instead* of fear and doom.

The fourth strategy I implemented was to develop the habit of focusing on positive words throughout the day.

I was desperate and overcome with fear and discouragement when I was so sick before my surgery in 2017. The enemy was filling my head with all kinds of lies and thoughts of scarcity. I remember thinking I needed to redirect my thoughts and get them turned toward God's truth, his promises, instead of my circumstances. Especially when my mind was "having a mind of its own."

I found Scriptures that resonated with me to shift my mind from fear to abundance. I love the Bible verse that says if we *hope* for what we don't see, we eagerly wait for it with patience (Romans 8:25 AMP). I also like the verse that reminds me to always be *thankful*, regardless of my circumstances (1 Thessalonians 5:18). And last, a Scripture that reminds me that God is always at work for my good, even if I don't see the good yet, encourages me to be *optimistic* (Romans 8:28).

Like my word for the year, I chose three specific words to represent those verses and reflect on—*hopeful, thankful, optimistic*. When I repeat these three words to myself, it helps me set my mind back to the truth. I can redirect my thoughts from negative to positive—

not lies like the enemy wanted me to think. At any point of the day, when I feel like I'm falling back into old habits, I recall those words and repeat them to remind me of the truth they represent. I still speak those words often.

My last strategy is to start each day by reminding myself that God has given me yet another day, and I'm thankful for the opportunity to live it with him (Psalm 118:24).

I try to do that the moment I open my eyes every morning. This discipline immediately gives me a sense of gratitude and joy. It sets my mind right, regardless of how I slept, how I feel, or what's in store for me that day.

Yes, this is the day the Lord has made. It may seem too simple a strategy, and I admit that there are some days when I don't feel so great when I do it, but as I've said before, there's power in the Word of God. Starting your day with this verse or another verse of your choosing helps set the tone before your mind has a chance to begin its chatter.

As I reflect on that fateful trip back to North Carolina and on to the White House, I know I could spend time kicking myself for not getting a handle on fear and making this trip sooner. But I'm reassured over and over again that things happen in God's timing and in his ways. What happened during those thirty-five years shaped my character, which made the trip and the outcome of my prayers even sweeter.

I wish I could say that I no longer feel fear, but I've realized that spreading fear is an effective tactic of the enemy. He never grows tired of using it, so we'll always have to face it. He loves to throw fear in the mix of a situation and stir things up over and over again—to throw me back into a mindset of scarcity and fear rather than abundance and goodness. But here's the difference now: I'm beginning to recognize it, realize who is doing it, and fight like hell against fear when it happens.

You see, our minds are often where much of the battle is fought. We think fearful thoughts, we feel fear, we're afraid of what might happen, so we don't do whatever we're prompted to do. Once I understood where fear is from—and that it's not from God—it became something tangible I could identify and fight against. And you can fight it too.

When I returned from my trip, I heard a song by Jesus Culture, "Show Me Your Glory."[5] I'd heard it many times over the years, but the lyrics really caught my attention this time. You might wonder what God's glory means. The glory of God is when his power, his divinity, his goodness, his love are displayed in some way. It could be through an event, a person, or nature—there are endless ways. For me, during that week in October 2018, God's glory was shown over and over to me—ceremonies, granite and bronze, written and spoken words, "chance" encounters, buildings on a campus, music, a joke, family, old friends and new, a photograph, a hug from a stranger, candlelight, a sunrise, and even a Facebook group—his power, goodness, love for me, and divine nature were evident throughout the week.

"Your glory surrounds me, and I'm overwhelmed. I'm not afraid. I'm not afraid. Show me your glory, show me your glory."[6]

These lyrics resonate with me. God is bigger than any fear that you or I will ever have. So my prayer is that as you battle with your worries, you won't be overwhelmed by the enemy or thoughts of scarcity and fear. Instead, you'll be overwhelmed by God's glory as he displays to you the abundance he's planned for each of us who love him.

---

[5] "Show Me Your Glory – Jesus Culture" on Grace Unlimited YouTube channel, uploaded January 16, 2019, https://www.youtube.com/watch?v=tuB6VSRcLG4.
[6] "Show Me Your Glory – Jesus Culture."

Insights and Scriptures to Adopt an Abundance Mindset
EVERYDAY APPLICATIONS

What I learned:

1. Change my mind to change my thinking habits. When I think about fear, I feel fear. There's biblical support and scientific evidence of this.

2. Understand my fear. This helps me deal with my fear. Ask questions like, What is it? Where is it coming from?

3. Take control of my thoughts by actively taking them captive. I can interrupt my thought patterns and replace them with God's truth.

4. Journal about my fears. Get them out of my head and onto paper and write down God's truth that disputes the fear. This helps me make sense of my emotions.

5. Expect good and abundance *instead* of fear and doom. Never expecting good is a hopeless way to live.

6. Don't borrow trouble. Stop the "what if" future thinking.

7. Focus on Scriptures and Word reminders to help me reset my mind, especially when I make them simple, easy, and quick to recall.

8. Every day is a blessing. Choose a favorite Scripture to reflect on as I wake up. This practice sets the tone of my day.

Scriptures that led me to these insights:

- For the Spirit God gave us does not make us timid, but gives us power, love and self-discipline. (2 Timothy 1:7)

- For as he thinks in his heart, so is he. (Proverbs 23:7 NKJV)

- And we take captive every thought and make it obedient to Christ. (2 Corinthians 10:5)
- For the despondent, every day brings trouble; for the happy heart, life is a continual feast. (Proverbs 15:15 NLT)
- But if we hope for what we do not see, we wait eagerly for it with patience and composure. (Romans 8:25 AMP)
- Give thanks in all circumstances, for this is God's will for you in Christ Jesus. (1 Thessalonians 5:18)
- And we know that in all things God works for the good of those who love him, who have been called according to his purpose. (Romans 8:28)
- This is the day that the LORD has made; let us rejoice and be glad in it. (Psalm 118:24 ESV)

Chapter 12

INSIGHT 9: REFLECT FOR LIFE LESSONS

As I reflect on my life's challenges, I often wonder: if I had to do it all over again, would I handle things differently? What would I tell someone else who was in similar shoes? What would be of benefit to you as you're reading this?

If I could give advice to my younger self, there are three things that I feel strongly would've changed the trajectory of my life much sooner. If you're trying to work through your own unresolved pains, I hope these help you on your path toward healing.

1. Know God.
2. Know yourself.
3. Find support.

Let's take these in order.

My first piece of advice is to know God. My relationship with the Lord has been crucial in my journey. The turning point in my faith was when it transitioned from the ritual and practices of religion to include a deep and personal relationship with God. God became man—Jesus Christ—human like us but perfect in every way. Once I grasped that I could have an intimate connection with God through Jesus Christ, like I have with other people, that became my saving grace.

I wish I had developed a deeper relationship with God sooner in my life. Although a religious lifestyle was modeled to me as a child, I wish the relational aspect of faith had also been modeled. I believed in God, but I didn't engage in a one-on-one relationship with him until well into my adult life. That wasn't God's fault (or anyone else's, for that matter.) It was mine. I chose to distance myself. But, as I drew near to God, he drew near to me (James 4:8), and God became an integral part of my day-to-day life.

The sooner your relationship with the Lord is in order, the better. Include him now, right this minute. Even if you don't currently believe in God or have a relationship with him, I strongly urge you to do something about that. There is no reason to face this life alone with whatever you're going through. Seek out a believer, or talk with a pastor.

Believing in God is the first step, but a relationship with him is more than that. It means you have to *pursue him and get to know him.* It takes time and commitment—just like you'd invest time and commitment in getting to know a new friend.

So how do you get to know God? You spend time with him. You can have an honest conversation with him (and listen) through prayer and consistently reading his Word. Don't push that responsibility to your pastor, priest, or someone else. *You* read the Bible for *yourself.* The words are meant for you. While biblical scholars are valuable teachers, no one else—no one in the history of the world—will read the Bible with your combination of experiences and perspective. How you read and understand his Word is unique to you, and no one can do it for you. Obviously there is tremendous merit in Bible scholars and theologians to help us grow our knowledge and understanding. But they don't replace your responsibility to read the Bible yourself.

I recommend not only reading the Bible but studying it—dig deep—understand what it says. Ask yourself questions like: What does this Scripture say? What does it mean in the context of the setting, culture, circumstances? How can it apply to my life today? Utilize tools such as study Bibles or online Bible commentaries (bibleref.com, biblehub.com, for example) to provide in-depth explanations, maps, diagrams and more to help you have a deeper study experience.

The Bible, inspired by God, has been in existence for thousands of years. It is consistent. It is relevant. It is alive and timeless (Hebrews 4:12 ESV). Through his Word, you can know who God is, his character traits, his promises, and how he wants you to live a life that's pleasing to him.

The world tells us such confusing and conflicting advice about living our lives. Today's "truth" will change tomorrow according to whatever fad or trend is in play. God's Word teaches us what is true, helps us know what is wrong, and trains us to do what is right. It is a trustworthy source that can be your guide and your compass.

In addition to knowing God through reading the Bible, it is crucial to stay consistently connected to God, to abide in him, throughout each day. I love the imagery in John 15:5 depicting God as a vine and us as the branches. Branches can't live independently of the vine. They have to be connected to the vine to thrive and bear fruit.

The same holds true for us and our relationship with God. I don't know about you, but I'd much rather stay tethered to the Lord and have the potential to bear fruit than be left to my own devices (John 15:6)—I've been there, and it was a very lonely, confusing, dark time in my life.

There are also many ways to stay consistently connected with the Lord. What has worked for me is some type of daily spiritual discipline consisting of Bible reading and prayer—and it doesn't have to be some massive block of time.

We have ninety-six individual fifteen-minute increments each day. How about giving God one of those? Give it a whirl, and see what happens over the next thirty days.

I crave my quiet time with the Lord, and I look forward to it each morning when I wake up. That daily time with God grounds me, inspires me, and often provides me new perspectives on issues I'm currently wrestling with. I start my day in a place of peace, knowing God is with me. I've even noticed that when I skip these times, my patience and peace are just not the same. If mornings are the most hectic part of your day, then choose another time. Maybe you want to spend fifteen minutes before you go to bed, or on your lunch hour, or in the pickup line at your kid's school. You get to choose.

However, staying connected extends beyond a daily quiet time. If you're like me, you can get going on your day, and, before you know it, the entire day has flown by and you realize you may not have thought about God outside of those fifteen minutes with him in the morning.

I realized I needed some God-reminders throughout the day. So I've placed favorite Bible verses and reminders in my home, car, and even on my phone. You can really get creative here. Phone alarms, screensavers, Post-it notes with Scripture are just a few examples. I also like to listen to Christian music in my car (The Message on SiriusXM, for example) and occasionally listen to podcasts (*The Proverbs 31 Ministries Podcast* and *Your Move with Andy Stanley Podcast*, for example). The world will try to distract you, so do what you can to stay connected to God with whatever reminders make sense for you. The result is that you'll stay connected and bear fruit for him.

Another step in the process of knowing God is to believe what he says. In Chapter 5, "Believe God," I wrote that it's important to reach a point in your faith journey where you *believe* his promises even when your circumstances are difficult. That's what faith is all about.

I realize that's sometimes really hard to do. I still struggle with it from time to time, but I have so many faithful role models to follow in the Bible: Abraham, Joseph, Moses, Esther, and Mary the mother of Jesus, just to name a few. Each had their own set of trials, and they all stayed faithful to God regardless of their circumstances. That's what we're called to do as well.

If I had to do it all over again, I'd start my journey with God *first, always.* I'd really get to know him and know his Word and stay closely connected to him all day, every day.

But if your story is like mine, and your journey didn't initially include a personal relationship with God, it's never too late to get started. Just start.

My second piece of advice is to know yourself. Just like it takes time to get to know God or any new friend, spend time really getting to know you. Do the work of self-awareness and self-discovery. It may be hard work at times, and this is another thing that no one can do for you, but you can achieve deep personal and spiritual transformation if you take the time.

I love the verse in 2 Corinthians 5:17 ESV, which tells us that we are a new creation in Christ when we begin our personal relationship with Jesus. Our old life has gone, and our new life has begun. But what I found in my personal experience was that my new creation was buried underneath my personality and all the pain I chose to suppress.

I realized I'd never be the true me until I knew myself, my character traits, and my habits and dealt with all the hurts I had buried. Until I did this work, I couldn't be the Theresa that God planned for me to be.

You may be saying, "I just don't have time." I get that, and I lived that for so many years. It's so easy to get lost in the hustle and bustle of life—especially if you're married and have kids. Raising a family, no matter what role you play, takes up a lot of time, and by the time you take care of everyone else, there isn't much time left to invest in yourself.

That was the trap I fell into for much of my adult life. I ran from one activity and one challenge or difficulty to the next. It wasn't until I was about to be an empty nester that I realized I had no clue who Theresa—the individual—really was. Don't use your busyness as an excuse. Knowing yourself is essential. Make the time.

Yes, I was Theresa. That's my name. But at the beginning of my healing journey, I saw myself as mainly "David's wife," "Dylan's mom," and "Tyler's mom." Not so much as just "Theresa." I started asking lots of questions: Who am I? Where is my identity? Why do I do the things I do? Why can't I get past my past circumstances?

That's how I began to look at *me*—not the world's definition of me, but just at me. That's how I began to understand what makes me tick. That's how I began to develop the courage to address parts of my life that I chose to run from.

I started looking within to understand who I really was, to understand my subconscious beliefs and behaviors that literally have a life of their own sometimes, and to get a handle on why I think the way I think, do the things I do, react the way I do, and hate conflict.

I used "that's just how I'm wired" for the longest time as my reason for my behaviors, but that's a cop-out. Just because we act a certain way, that doesn't mean we can't change to be a better version of ourselves—to be more like Christ. Yeah, I may hate conflict, but that doesn't mean it's okay for me to avoid it. No, that's an excuse.

As part of my journey, I've taken several personality tests and assessments. Myers-Briggs Type Indicator, CliftonStrengths assessment (formerly known as StrengthsFinder), and DiSC® assessment were just a few that I took. Each helped me know more about myself. They gave me frameworks to see things I was blind to.

Then I was introduced to the Enneagram, and I began to understand *why* I do the things I do. The Enneagram breaks personalities into nine types. We each have parts of all nine, but everyone has a dominant type that reveals our natural strengths and difficulties. I realized that my fear of conflict and ignoring my feelings were similar to Type 9—The Peacemaker. Avoiding conflict is a key motivator for Type 9 because of the innate desire to maintain peace. This inclination to avoid conflict often causes them to ignore their feelings and evade emotional issues. Sound familiar?

Thankfully, there are many strengths of The Peacemaker that I also saw in myself, like being highly empathetic, having the ability to see all sides, and being inclusive. Understanding all these qualities gave me some comfort. I finally had explanations to some of the questions I struggled with and could move past the why.

What I love about the Enneagram is that it's a tool to help you understand yourself as you are and then help you move toward growth—to get to the true *you* underneath all the false beliefs and behaviors you've acquired and understand the unhealthy side while showing you how to move toward a healthy version of yourself.

I was motivated to become God's new creation and let the old version of me go. I needed to understand what part was old and begin to move past it, and these tools helped me do that.

I learned to use the Enneagram purely as a tool for self-awareness—not as a shield or a sword. In other words, I don't use my type to excuse my behaviors or actions. Nor do I use it to attack myself—or others. Using it to defend or blame is misusing this tool, and I caution you against doing that.

If you're interested in knowing more, I highly recommend Ian Cron's IEQ9 Enneagram test, his Typology Institute, and *Typology* podcast, as well as Beth and Jeff McCord's book *Becoming Us*[1] and their *Your Enneagram Coach* podcast. I follow them on Instagram as well, @yourenneagramcoach, and I find that their posts are great reminders and encouragement.

Regardless of the tools you use, please take the time to

---

[1] Beth McCord, Jeff McCord, *Becoming Us: Using the Enneagram to Create a Thriving Gospel-Centered Marriage* (New York: Morgan James Publishing, 2020).

understand yourself. Your self-awareness, self-esteem, compassion, and appreciation for yourself will grow, and your ability to embrace others and their differences will grow as well.

My third piece of advice is to find support if you're struggling. Don't go it alone. Since I stuffed my pain and chose to hide from it, I didn't seek any help for decades.

I hoped that time would heal it all. But, in my experience, time doesn't heal all wounds. I believe growth can heal, but growth is sometimes hard to experience when you're alone in your journey and trying to figure out everything on your own. So save yourself some heartache, and find support.

Humans are created for community. Support can come from friends, family, coworkers, peers, and fellow Christians. But there are so many other options, and here are a few:

If you're struggling with grief, anger, bitterness, or other difficult emotions, seek a pastor or a licensed counselor or therapist. Personally, I found great benefit from a counselor with a Christian background who leaned on both his expertise and his faith when providing wisdom and counsel. They can help you unpack any difficult emotions that you're struggling with while also being aligned with biblical principles.

If you've experienced a death or a significant loss in your life, seek out grief support. I'll never understand why that wasn't recommended to me nor why I didn't look into it myself. Don't make that same mistake I made. I know the world wants those who grieve to just get over it and put on a happy face, but that's not how it works. Instead, walk through it. Grief has a beginning and an end.

A book I like to recommend is *Experiencing Grief*[2] by H. Norman Wright. This practical guide explains grief and walks through the process. It's divided into digestible sections and is an easy read.

Even though I read it years after John's death, I found it enlightening and helpful on my healing journey.

---

[2] H. Norman Wright, *Experiencing Grief* (Nashville: B&H Publishing Group, 2004).

Another option to build your support team is to find a spiritual mentor. A spiritual mentor is someone who is a bit farther along in his or her faith journey than you. Your mentor can walk alongside you to help you stay biblically grounded and provide biblical insight into your struggles. This person can also be an excellent source for prayer, support, and accountability. I wish I had a mentor as a young person.

If you're interested in finding a spiritual mentor, contact your church ministry team. See if they have a discipleship or mentoring program to connect with, or share this desire with your pastor.

If you want to better understand yourself and want help setting and achieving goals, I'd highly recommend using a life coach. Whereas a therapist will focus on your past or present, a life coach focuses on the present and the future.

There was a time early in my journey when I met with a personal coach for several months. It was a beneficial process that I leaned on as I transitioned to my current season as an empty nester. I really dug into understanding my strengths, weaknesses, values, and desires and was able to home in on an overall purpose for my life going forward. It has been helpful even as I write this book.

Most importantly, don't go it alone. Life can be challenging. We thrive and flourish when we have people who support us on our journeys. Be intentional about building your team. It won't create itself. It's okay if you don't choose people who are considered "natural" supports on your team, like family or friends, because you're not comfortable or they aren't supportive and may even impair your growth. Only you can be the judge of that. The key is to select people you can trust and feel safe to be vulnerable and honest with.

There is great wisdom in the book of Proverbs about having many advisers in our lives and listening to counsel for our plans to succeed (Proverbs 15:22 ESV). God knows that when left to our own devices, we can all go in the wrong direction. Personally, I believe it's prudent to surround yourself with wise and godly people to accompany you on your life journey and process with you as you tackle life's ups and downs. It may not be practical to have a counselor, coach, or mentor simultaneously. Still, you may find it helpful to seek guidance from each at different points in your life.

Each of us is on our own journey while we're here on Earth, and we know that part of that journey will involve difficulties (John 16:33). Being intentional to equip yourself so that you don't get stuck when you experience hard times is key.

Now I have the benefit of hindsight, and when looking back I found that as I've grown to know God, understood myself better, and found support along this journey, I've gained new perspectives to address my past hurts and fears and move forward to the new creation God intended for me.

I want that for you, as well.

Insights and Scriptures to Reflect for Life Lessons
EVERYDAY APPLICATIONS

What I learned:

1. Know God. Know myself. Find support.

2. Knowing God starts with a personal relationship with God through his Son, Jesus. Knowing *about* God is not enough. Draw near to him and make him an integral part of my life.

3. Know God by reading his Word. It's up to me to read the Bible for myself rather than only relying on the wisdom and interpretations of other people—including priests or pastors.

4. God's Word is timeless, relevant, and trustworthy. With all that is ever-changing, the Word of God is constant. It's my compass and my guide throughout my life.

5. Stay connected to God throughout the day, like branches are to a vine. Suggestions include daily and consistent quiet time, prayer, and reminders throughout my day.

6. Believe God and his promises. Don't just believe *in* him. Faith is believing God and his promises even when my circumstances are challenging.

7. To know myself means doing the work of self-discovery and self-awareness. That process allows me to uncover what may be keeping me from being all that God wants me to be. This work can sometimes be hard, but it's always rewarding.

8. There are lots of resources available for self-discovery. Myers-Briggs Type Indicator, DiSC® assessment, CliftonStrengths assessment, and the Enneagram are just a few. Whatever tools I choose, the point is to take time to understand myself and grow from it.

9. Find support. I am created for community. Find people to support me on my journey. Be intentional. Options may include friends, family, pastors, licensed counselors/therapists, spiritual mentors, and life coaches. Don't go it alone.

Scriptures that led me to these insights:

- Come near to God, and he will come near to you. (James 4:8)

- For the word of God is living and active, sharper than any two-edged sword, piercing to the division of soul and of spirit, of joints and of marrow, and discerning the thoughts and intentions of the heart. (Hebrews 4:12 ESV)

- I am the vine; you are the branches. If you remain in me and I in you, you will bear much fruit; apart from me you can do nothing. (John 15:5)

- If you do not remain in me, you are like a branch that is thrown away and withers; such branches are picked up, thrown into the fire, and burned. (John 15:6)

- Therefore, if anyone is in Christ, he is a new creation. The old has passed away; behold, the new has come. (2 Corinthians 5:17 ESV)

- Without counsel, plans fail, but with many advisers, they succeed. (Proverbs 15:22 ESV)

- I have told you these things, so that in me you may have peace. In this world, you will have trouble. But take heart! I have overcome the world. (John 16:33)

Epilogue

GOD IS ALWAYS WORKING FOR OUR GOOD

As I reflect on that tragic moment in my life in 1983 and the subsequent challenges, I've come to realize that God was working to bring good out of all the difficulties I faced. Even in moments when his hand and presence were not apparent to me, his purpose was unfolding for my ultimate well-being.

I'm reminded of the story of Joseph and his brothers in the book of Genesis. Joseph, son of Jacob, had been left for dead by his brothers. He was sold into slavery and imprisoned for many years. Later, Joseph became second in command in Egypt. During that time, Joseph found himself face-to-face again with his brothers. When they realized it was Joseph, they began begging him for his forgiveness. Despite all that had happened, he replied with profound words, "As for you, you meant evil against me, but God meant it for good to bring about this present outcome." (Genesis 50:20 AMP).

I think how God took my difficult circumstances and my inability to face my pain and turned them into something I can use to help others. As I ponder this, it takes my breath away.

As I healed, I learned many lessons and gained much needed insights and perspectives in the heat of battle. As a result, God has put on my heart to share those insights with *you*—to tell *you* all that he has done for me (Mark 5:19 NKJV). Whether that's through sharing my story with family or friends, mentoring other women, leading Bible studies, speaking to groups, or this book, it has become a calling for me. I now see how God has used it all for my good and to maybe help you with your healing journey, too.

As I sit with a finished book, my lessons haven't stopped. My healing journey continues. It's taken me more than three years to get down on paper what's been on my heart, and there have been times when I've totally stopped writing, ready to throw in the towel.

Who am I to share lessons and insights when I'm not finished learning, myself?

That's life, isn't it—a culmination of lots of lessons. It's through our experiences that we're molded to become more like Jesus, and we never finish learning. It's through telling our stories that we share how God has touched our lives, and how we perhaps help others on their journey and to know God.

We're all Christ's ambassadors, given an assignment on behalf of God, to tell others about him (2 Corinthians 5:20). I take that assignment seriously. This book is one way I'm doing that. I hope the stories and insights I shared encourage you. I hope they give you courage to process your own pain. I hope you will:

- be encouraged to begin your own journey of healing.
- know God more in the process.
- get the support that you want and deserve.
- have a keen sense of understanding of yourself and others.
- come to a place where you see and want to share all that God has done for you.

In the end, don't we all want to hear that God is pleased with us? Don't we all want to be told we've done a good job? Don't we want to ensure that more people know about him because we were bold enough to share our stories?

That's my desire. I hope it's yours, too.

Matthew 25:21 says, "His master replied, 'Well done, good and faithful servant! You have been faithful with a few things; I will put you in charge of many things. Come and share your master's happiness!' "

I assure you, God will be with you on this journey (Isaiah 41:10). To God be the glory.

Scriptures referenced in the epilogue:

- As for you, you meant evil against me, but God meant it for good in order to bring about this present outcome. (Genesis 50:20 AMP)

- However, Jesus did not permit him, but said to him, "Go home to your friends, and tell them what great things the Lord has done for you, and how He has had compassion on you." (Mark 5:19 NKJV)

- We are therefore Christ's ambassadors, as though God were making his appeal through us. We implore you on Christ's behalf: Be reconciled to God. (2 Corinthians 5:20)

- So do not fear, for I am with you; do not be dismayed, for I am your God. I will strengthen you and help you; I will uphold you with my righteous right hand. (Isaiah 41:10)

- His master replied, "Well done, good and faithful servant! You have been faithful with a few things; I will put you in charge of many things. Come and share your master's happiness!" (Matthew 25:21)

Appendix

ADDITIONAL RESOURCES FOR YOUR JOURNEY

Daily Quiet Time Resource Suggestions

In Chapter 4, I shared my practice of daily quiet time, nurturing my personal connection with God. Here, I offer a selection of resources that have supported me along this journey. Please note that this list is not exhaustive but serves as inspirational guidance.

BIBLES

- Life Application Study Bible—includes descriptions of context and setting, life application notes, charts, diagrams, maps, and more.

- Journaling Bible—includes wide margins on the side for taking notes when inspired while reading the Word.

ONLINE BIBLE RESOURCES

- YouVersion (https://www.youversion.com)—online Bible app that includes free access to multiple versions in multiple languages; also provides devotional plans.
- BibleGateway (https://www.biblegateway.com)—online searchable website that provides free access to multiple Bible versions in multiple languages.

ONLINE DEVOTIONALS

- First 5 Daily Bible Study App (https://first5.org)—provides online Bible study plans and access to multiple Bible versions.
- YouVersion (https://www.youversion.com)—provides free access to multiple devotional plans organized by topic in addition to multiple Bible versions.

PODCASTS

- *The Proverbs 31 Ministries Podcast*—shares biblical truth for women. Episodes include topics on leadership, spiritual growth, theology, navigating hard seasons, and more.
- *Your Move with Andy Stanley Podcast*—weekly messages from Andy Stanley, senior pastor, North Point Ministries, to discover how to make better decisions and fewer regrets.

PRAYER

- Prime Time with God (https://churchgrowth.org/ephesians-4-ministries/)—subscribe to daily prayer and devotional emails from Ephesians 4 Ministries.
- YouVersion (https://www.youversion.com)—in addition to

online Bible resources and devotional plans, the Daily Refresh feature provides guided prayer to step you through a four-to six-minute time of intentional prayer.

JOURNALING

Below are the types of journaling methods that I use. I follow one of these suggestions depending upon what is on my heart at the time, and I use a blank journal.

- Prayer—write out prayers along with any Bible verses that may come to mind.

- Gratitude—write down three to five things for which I am grateful that day.

- Scripture—keep a journal of key Scriptures that are meaningful to me.

- Thoughts and inspirations—record what is on my heart; include Scriptures that come to mind, wisdom from the Holy Spirit, and/or emotions that I may be experiencing.

Scripture Memorization Techniques

In Chapter 6, I discussed the importance of memorizing Scriptures to effectively fight the enemy. The techniques described below are a few ways I began to set meaningful Bible verses to memory.

1. Incrementally memorize Scripture.
   - Divide the verse into smaller "chunks."
   - Memorize each "chunk" one at a time.

2. Make Scripture mnemonics that help you easily remember.
   - For example, Philippians 4:8 says, "Whatever is true whatever is noble, whatever is right, whatever is pure whatever is lovely, whatever is admirable—if anything is excellent or praiseworthy—think about such things."

   - A sample mnemonic is "Theresa Never Really Puts Laundry Away Except Pants." It helps me to remember "true, noble right, pure, lovely, admirable, excellent." Silly but effective.

3. Write it multiple times.
   - The act of writing helps commit the verse to memory.
   - The visual image helps cement it into memory.

4. Say the verse out loud. This is especially helpful for audio learners.

5. Listen to the verse. Hearing the verse numerous times can help it stick.
   - Create a recording, or listen to the verse on an online Bible app like YouVersion (https://www.youversion.com).

6. Turn the verse into a song. My kids and I used to listen to

Bible verses set to music when they were young. To this day, we all can quote Philippians 4:6-7 by singing the song.

- Search for Scripture memory songs on Spotify or YouTube—listen and start singing.

7. Place the verse in visible places.

- Post-its
- Note cards

    - Put the notes on your mirror or computer monitor; put them in your car, bathroom, kitchen, wherever you go.

Ten Scriptures to Fight the Enemy

These are some of the verses that encourage me to keep fighting the enemy. They reassure me that God is always with me and that he comforts and strengthens me in my struggles.

1. And we know that in all things God works for the good of those who love him, who have been called according to his purpose. (Romans 8:28)

2. "For I know the plans I have for you," declares the Lord, "plans to prosper you and not to harm you, plans to give you hope and a future." (Jeremiah 29:11)

3. "Have I not commanded you? Be strong and courageous. Do not be afraid; do not be discouraged, for the Lord your God will be with you wherever you go." (Joshua 1:9)

4. "So do not fear, for I am with you; do not be dismayed, for I am your God. I will strengthen you and help you; I will uphold you with my righteous right hand." (Isaiah 41:10)

5. We demolish arguments and every pretension that sets itself up against the knowledge of God, and we take captive every thought to make it obedient to Christ. (2 Corinthians 10:5)

6. God is our refuge and strength, an ever-present help in trouble. (Psalm 46:1)

7. I can do all this through him who gives me strength. (Philippians 4:13)

8. Even youths grow tired and weary, and young men stumble and fall; but those who hope in the Lord will renew their strength. They will soar on wings like eagles; they will run and not grow weary; they will walk and not be faint. (Isaiah 40:30-31)

9. "Do not be afraid of them; the Lord your God himself will fight for you." (Deuteronomy 3:22)

10. Even though I walk through the darkest valley, I will fear no evil, for you are with me; your rod and your staff, they comfort me. (Psalm 23:4)

ACKNOWLEDGEMENTS

While writing and publishing this book, I've been blessed with the support of an incredible group of people who have played important roles along the way.

First and foremost, to God, who not only gave me the strength and courage to face my fears but also provided the profound insights that led me to hope and healing. His guidance and the perseverance he provided me to write and share this story were essential. All glory goes to him.

To my wonderful husband, David, your unwavering support has been constant throughout this entire journey. For over three decades of our marriage, you've expressed empathy and love without hesitation as I've wrestled with the aftermath of the tragic terrorist attack and its impact on me. Your gentle encouragement pushed me to face my deepest fears, urging me to return to where my tragedy began—Camp Lejeune—and later compelling me to write this book and share my story. Your role as my encourager and cheerleader has never wavered. Thank you for being my partner, my rock, and my confidant as I've brought this book to life.

To my mom, Lucile, your support and presence in my darkest

hours were an anchor during such a traumatic time. Forty years later, at 98, your presence is a precious gift, allowing me to share this book with you in person. Thank you for being a model of strength, courage, and perseverance.

To my sons, Dylan and Tyler, this book is my legacy to you—giving you a deeper understanding of my journey, my struggles, and the insights I learned. Tyler, your profound question, "What will you think about yourself in twenty years if you don't finish the book?" pushed me forward. And, Dylan, your constant empathy and advice as a fellow creator eased my countless doubts throughout this writing process.

To my daughter-in-law, Bethany, when my tank was empty, your support in the final stages was a lifeline. Thank you for handling many details, large and small.

Robyn Van Zandt, my cherished friend, your guidance as a professional life coach played a crucial role in my self-discovery as Theresa, the individual. You wisely encouraged me to do the hard work to uncover my life purpose, which ultimately led me to write this book to help other people and proclaim all that God has done for me.

Lynn Price, our chance meeting to learn that you published a book was a divine appointment. Our ongoing conversations early on motivated me to begin the writing process, and your wisdom—done is better than perfect—was a helpful reminder.

To Sue Jones, my walking buddy and dear friend, your heart to listen and your wisdom shared while walking hundreds of miles throughout this experience have been a constant encouragement.

Amy Knight, you challenged me to share my story in writing and paint my interpretation of the book title for the cover. I didn't think I had it in me to do both for this project, but God had a different idea.

My Bible study girlfriends—Nancy, Karen, Christine, Jane, Rhonda, Carol, Marci, and Missy—your tireless prayers sustained me throughout this long process.

ACKNOWLEDGEMENTS

Laura and Alexis, my mentees, your interest and encouragement as I worked on the manuscript and your excitement as I took each step toward a published book have been uplifting.

Angela Belford, reconnecting with you was serendipitous, and your experienced guidance through the publishing process was a true blessing. You and The Belford Group played a vital role in helping me get this book to the finish line.

Darinda Sharp, your editing prowess and insightful questions transformed this book. Your ability to edit and serve as a compassionate adviser, coaxing out more details of my story, has taken this book to new heights. As I wrestled with publicly sharing my story, I will forever remember your advice—own it.

Suzy Taylor Oakley, your meticulous proofreading is genuinely valued. Your tireless efforts and dedication have gone above and beyond in transforming my manuscript into its final book form, ensuring a reader-friendly experience.

Cedric Fonville, Durrell Green, Donna Garrett from Nice NWA, you provided an enjoyable experience and outstanding photography in the final stages of this project.

To everyone else who supported and motivated me to stay the course and finish writing my story, your encouragement and motivation were invaluable.

I am forever grateful to all of you for making this book possible.

ABOUT THE AUTHOR

B orn and raised in Georgia, Theresa Roth is not only an author but is a mentor and artist with a passion for sharing the transformative journey that God has led her through. Her mission is to comfort and encourage others to embark on their own path to hope and healing. Whether that's by sharing her story through this impactful book, speaking to groups, or mentoring individuals, it has become a calling for her.

With a business career spanning thirty-five years in the marketplace, Theresa held diverse management positions in consulting, marketing and communications, event planning, and finance. For twenty years, Theresa partnered with her husband, David, founder and former CEO of Workmatters, a nonprofit faith-and-work organization, serving in various roles.

Theresa and David reside in the heart of the beautiful Ozark Mountains in Fayetteville, Arkansas. They enjoy hiking, biking, canoeing, and spending time at the beach, the mountains, and in between. They are blessed with two wonderful adult sons, Dylan, his wife Bethany, and Tyler.

As she tells in *Facing Your Fears*, Theresa made a return trip to Camp Lejeune, NC, and Washington, DC, to commemorate the thirty-fifth anniversary of the Beirut bombing that claimed the lives of her first husband and 240 other servicemen. During those cere-monies, she was introduced to a motto, "The First Duty is to Re-member," which has been the catalyst for her to remember and honor those killed in this event and also to tell all that God has done for her in her own journey of healing.

In response to her calling to remember and tell, Theresa established the 1st Lt. John Boyett Memorial Leadership Scholarship Fund to honor the values of John Boyett. This is a merit-based scholarship for the Workmatters Institute and goes to deserving individuals who desire in-depth leadership and career development from a faith-based perspective. For more information, go to https://workmatters.org/scholarships.

To contact Theresa, please visit www.theresarothauthor.com.